BREXIT.
THE TIP OF THE
POPULIST ICEBERG?

J.N. PAQUET

- ESSAY -

BREXIT. THE TIP OF THE POPULIST ICEBERG?

Special thanks to Lu.

BREXIT. THE TIP OF THE POPULIST ICEBERG?

Brexit [noun] — 1. a British way out of the European Union. Examples: *"What is Brexit?"*, *"What does Brexit mean?"*, *"Brexit means Brexit."* **— 2.** the act of Britain leaving the European Union. Examples: *"The British people eventually voted for Brexit"*, *"The Prime minister resigned before Brexit actually started."*, *"The truth is that Brexit might never actually happen."*

Populism [noun] — 1. a type of politics that claims to represent the opinions and wishes of ordinary people. Example: *"Donald Trump espouses right-wing populism."* - **2.** a belief in the power of ordinary people and in their right to have control over their government rather than a small group of political insiders or a wealthy elite, who can be overthrown. Examples: *"Angry populism is the driving force of politics today."*

"My friends, as I have discovered myself,
there are no disasters, only opportunities.
And, indeed, opportunities for fresh disasters."

— Boris Johnson, 9 April 2012
(Newspaper column written in 2004)[1]

---

[1] From gaffes to glory, Boris keeps Britain guessing (09/04/2012, Reuters - https://goo.gl/cPj5xC)

***NOT* ANOTHER BOOK ABOUT BREXIT.**

"What Mr Wilders shares in common with Mr Trump, Mr Orban, Mr Zeman, Mr Hofer, Mr Fico, Madame Le Pen, Mr Farage, he also shares with Da'esh. All seek to recover a past, halcyon and so pure in form, where sunlit fields are settled by peoples united by ethnicity or religion – living peacefully in isolation, pilots of their fate, free of crime, foreign influence and war. A past that most certainly, in reality, did not exist anywhere, ever. The proposition of recovering a supposedly perfect past is fiction; its merchants are cheats."

These were the words of Prince Zeid Ra'ad al-Hussein, the United Nations High Commissioner for Human Rights, who branded Western populist politicians *"demagogues and political fantasists"* at a security conference in The Hague, on 5 September 2016.[2]

In this book, we will take a close look at the dynamics

---

[2] Zeid warns against populists and demagogues in Europe and U.S. (05/09/2016, UN's OHCHR - http://goo.gl/uHHuFh)

that exist between populism and the society in general. From Nigel Farage in Britain to Podemos in Spain, Syriza in Greece, Sarkozy, Orbán, Hofer or Duda, the book takes us on a journey to understand how populist characters have successfully challenged established elites, mainstream parties and experts in recent years and forever redefined politics from a Left-Right two-party system with shared democratic values to a split multi-party system with deeply rooted nationalistic and revolutionary principles. The old Left-Right, Socialist-Conservative, Labour-Tories and Democrats-Republicans divisions have now given place to new divides: Brexiteers-Remoaners, Trump-Sanders, Racists/Bigoted-World Citizens, Populists-Unifiers.

For the last few decades or so, in many countries across the globe, people have been tempted by the populist vote with promises of more democracy, less corruption, more transparency, more reforms, fewer elites, fewer experts and more power to the people (*"Take back control"* was the motto of the Leave campaigners during the British EU Referendum campaign, whilst *"Make America great again"* was Trump's motto). But how has it actually materialised, so far?

This is not "yet another book about Brexit and the EU referendum". It is not about whether one side was right and the other wrong. This book is about populism. It will explain whether the British EU referendum result will have any impact on the United Kingdom only, or further across the pond. It matters because its potential impact could change the lives of millions of people, if not billions, all around the world, whether economically, politically, or geopolitically.

This series will report on the way populism has been spreading so far in the world in recent years and try to find the facts that might illustrate whether the populist trend is still spreading or finally coming to a slowdown, even a halt.

This first volume will focus on populism in Europe. The next three volumes will report on the Americas, the rest of the world and conclude with the United Kingdom.

J.N. PAQUET

VOLUME I

THE CURRENT STATE OF POPULISM IN EUROPE

BREXIT MEANT BREXIT.

- **Country:** Great Britain

- **Eligible to vote:** 46,420,413 (2015)

- **Next General election:** 7 May 2020

- **GDP:** $2.858 trillion (2015 est.)

- **Public debt:** 89% of GDP (2015 est.)

- **Unemployment:** 5.4% (2015)

- **Population below poverty line:** 15% (2013 est.)

- **Inflation rate:** 0.1% (2015 est.)

(Source: The CIA World Factbook) [3]

KEY NAMES:

- **Nigel Farage,** MEP, former leader of the United Kingdom Independence Party (UKIP), a far-right political party.

- **Boris Johnson,** UK Foreign Secretary,

---

[3] The World Factbook - France (Central Intelligence Agency - https://goo.gl/jV1epw)

Conservative MP and former Mayor of London.

- **Theresa May,** UK Prime Minister, leader of the Conservative Party.

For some people in Britain, before 23 June 2016, populist politicians like Nigel Farage were nothing but comets crossing the political orbit every century or so, and whose actual influence on politics would always be deemed both insignificant and inconsequential. That was before the EU referendum took place.

Farage was no comet. The Brexit vote was no accident. A combination of unfortunate factors and events eventually led to the 23 June vote that resulted in the Brexit win. Everyone now accepts, for instance, that the senior campaigners in favour of the Remain vote, during the British EU referendum campaign, were perceived by the public as the "Project Fear" team (representing the establishment, the elites, the economic notability and their so-called experts) and their fearful language somehow discredited them, whilst the Leave vote campaigners used a largely populist rhetoric, claiming that THEY were speaking up for ordinary working people and THEY were defending them against the fat-cats. Fifty-two per cent of the British voters believed them.

Could Brexit and its accurately-predicted catastrophic

outcome (dropping currency, global market losses, loss of economic confidence and threats of job and investment losses) be the final drop that will change the way people vote for the decades to come in Europe and, to some extent maybe, all over the world? Or could it actually broaden the populists' message of widespread insecurity, mass immigration, and economic crisis, and make it even stronger than ever before, thanks to the likes of Nigel Farage and Donald Trump, the Machiavels and Mephistopheles of the twenty-first century?

Was Brexit only the tip of the populist iceberg? Are there any other underlying reasons why the populist vote is trending across Europe and in America, whilst Latin America is going the opposite direction and turning its back to populism? More generally, what makes people vote for populist politicians such as Jeremy Corbyn, Bernie Sanders, Nigel Farage, or Donald Trump? What makes them serious contenders compared to other mainstream politicians?

Nigel Farage.

Nigel Farage has been a key player of team UKIP for over 24 years and its captain for the last ten years, before leading the team one last time to victory last June when UKIP won the "Brexit Championship Final". Farage is currently available on a free transfer this autumn and it would be very surprising if the Tories weren't keen to tempt the player with a new challenge back in the team that saw him start his career over 30 years ago.

A skilful populist and smart politician, the impatient Nigel Farage knows that the best way to get what he wants is actually... to be patient. Very patient. First, he must be thankful to his supporters and pretend that it's the end (it clearly is the end of UKIP, just not the end of his political career yet): *"I am still four-square behind this party and its aims"*, *"I've done my bit"*, *"I want my life back"*. Then he must adopt a low-profile. A very low profile. He must keep away from the media for a while to come back as a saviour, a hero. Britain loves its heroes.

And indeed, Nigel Farage gave a speech at the European Freedom Awards on 4 November 2016, in Stockholm (a meeting of European nationalists), in which he warned: *"If Brexit doesn't mean Brexit, I'll be back in 2019. And probably with a pitchfork!"*

At the quite odd ceremony, Nigel Farage explained that if the High Court ruling that the British Parliament must vote on Article 50 was used to delay "his" Brexit and *"if there is any attempt to water it down, to kick it into the long grass, the British people will not put up with it, and I will myself return from this very quiet period of my life, this retirement that I'm going through."*

Nigel Farage threatening to come back is one thing the British public has been used to living with for a while. He resigns as leader, then comes back as leader. He claims he lost the referendum, then says he won it. He resigns as leader again, gets replaced by someone who resigns too, then he comes back and goes again.

As for the quiet retirement Farage mentioned...[4] Since the Brexit vote, Nigel Farage has been seen at the Republican National Convention in Cleveland, appeared with his new presidential mate Donald Trump at Trump's political rallies and to coach him before his debate with Hillary Clinton, gave interviews to various American TV channels about Trump and Brexit (including to conspiracy theory channel Infowars) – let's not forget that memorable photograph with Donald in front of the golden lift inside the Trump Tower, appeared on Russian TV channel RT at various times with and without moustache, appeared on *60 Minutes Australia*, appeared on Andrew Marr's, Robert Peston's and Andrew Neil's shows, on *Good Morning Britain* and *Loose Women*, had (and still has) his own weekly show on *LBC* and appeared on his super mate Nick Ferrari's *LBC Breakfast* show week after week for months in the run-up to the EU referendum, showed up at the European Parliament to insult the other MEPs, etc.

---

4 Nigel Farage: "I'll Be Back... in 2019!" (05/11/2016, Byline - https://goo.gl/sebhGC)

Believe it or not, Nigel Farage is very far from retiring from politics.

Boris Johnson.

Some people had a deep reason to wish for the UK to leave the European Union, whether it was a frustration at the way the European institutions work, or the way they feel Brussels gives the orders and Britain just obeys, or maybe it is because they feel the government has no power to limit EU immigration...

These reasons, whether right or wrong, are things real Eurosceptics feel deep in their heart. They dislike the EU, they cannot stand the idea of "ever closer union", they just hate the idea of losing the pound. It is a deep inward feeling, something literally visceral rather than subject to their personal ambitions. That is why they are usually good fits for TV debates and get invited to give their opinion on the EU and throw at the audience some impassioned speeches that will upset some and make others happy.

Fair enough. Everyone can and should have a say. We live in a democracy and there is such a thing as freedom of speech after all. The likes of UKIP leader Nigel Farage or Tory MP Jacob Rees-Mogg, to name just a few well-known Eurosceptics who have been battling against the European Union for a very long time and are never short of harsh attacks on the EU and the "failures" of its institutions, may have an opinion one totally disagrees with, but they have not suddenly changed their minds for the sake of a career move that could lead them to a seat in the cabinet or a top position offered for their loyalty to some donors or senior figures within the "Leave the EU" campaign.

Evelyn Beatrice Hall, famously misquoting Voltaire, wrote *"I disapprove of what you say, but I will defend to the death your right to say it"*, which absolutely applied to the debate.

The debate on Britain's EU membership, however, posed a question that was not whether the UK should remain in or leave the European Union, but whether some politicians would dare put their personal agenda before the interests of a nation and therefore hijack a referendum campaign because they dreamt of the top job that could become vacant, providing David Cameron would fail to convince the British people that the UK should remain in the European Union. And he badly did!

Boris Johnson, however, did not have the interest of the United Kingdom in mind. The former Mayor of London had repeatedly praised and celebrated the benefits the UK's membership of the EU brings to London. In 2009, for instance, Boris Johnson praised the European Investment Bank (EIB) for granting London a £1 billion loan for the Crossrail project.[5]

At the time, Johnson said: *"Our good friends at the EIB have provided us with a billion more reasons to proceed with the unstoppable force that is Crossrail. It is one of the largest loans ever secured for a transport project and I am especially pleased to have this backing for our drive to provide London with the facilities required to keep the capital one of the world's leading cities."*

Not only is it absurd and selfish to bury one's beliefs in order to fulfil one's ambition, but it also says a lot about the way one can be expected to run a city or represent a constituency, let alone... run a country.

After the Brexit vote, Theresa May asked Boris Johnson to become her Foreign secretary. This is a position in which one must show diplomatic skills. Skills Boris Johnson unfortunately doesn't have, as he repeatedly proved it in the past, and proves it again and again, with him recently saying Saudi Arabia is a 'puppeteer' in the Middle East proxy wars, for instance.[6]

---

[5] Crossrail secures £1bn loan from European Investment Bank (08/09/2009, The Guardian - https://goo.gl/IRV1LY)
[6] Johnson says Saudi Arabia is a 'puppeteer' in Middle East proxy wars (08/12/2016, The Guardian - https://goo.gl/htzpXX)

Alex Taylor
@AlexTaylorNews

@BorisJohnson @GiselaStuart admit to standing in front of the Brexit bus with a HUGE LIE.
independent.co.uk/news/uk/politi …

We send the EU £350 millior
let's fund our NHS instead
Let's t   ontrol

12:07 pm - 12 Sep 2016

Theresa May.

Theresa May has a hidden master plan for Brexit: let the Brexiteers talk about what they think Brexit must be and share their ideas in public, in the press, in conferences and as loud as possible, then undermine them afterwards by claiming that they are not talking on behalf of the government but merely expressing their views. She did so with David Davis, Liam Fox, and Boris Johnson.

By undermining them and ridiculing their efforts at defining a hardcore Brexit, Theresa May reminds everyone that she is the Prime Minister and that only she will eventually decide what Brexit means. Thus, the Brexit ministers will be seen as incompetent by the British public and an easy target to blame if everything goes wrong when trying to negotiate Britain's exit from the European Union.

Is Theresa May a populist politician? She does know how to make people hear what she wants them to hear. She can tell people that the Labour Party is now the "nasty party" and it somehow sounds true. She tells people *"Brexit means Brexit"* and people believe her, even though nobody actually knows what Brexit means.

Theresa May has a special talent that the Farage, Boris and co. don't have: she has the style and the talk that fit the position of Prime Minister. She could well not be very efficient at all, but nobody would question her efficiency. She is self-confident too. The most successful populist characters match the can with the will.

We will report more on the state of populism in Great Britain in Volume 4 of this series, *Populism in Britain*, with a stronger insight on how Brexit will have developed one year on. The book will be published on 23 June 2017 on the anniversary date of the EU referendum.

HarperCollinsUK
@HarperCollinsUK

Follow

BREXIT has been revealed as the 2016 Collins Word of the Year #CollinsWOTY

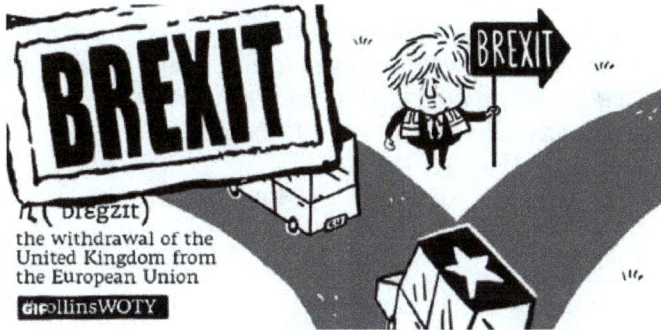

BREXIT

(ˈbrɛgzɪt)
the withdrawal of the
United Kingdom from
the European Union

CollinsWOTY

RETWEETS   LIKES
31   26

9:09 AM - 3 Nov 2016

City of London, London

31   26

* * *

"I'm getting a bit tired of my kids coming home from school being taught about every other religion in the world, celebrating every other religious holiday, but not actually being taught about Christianity."

— Nigel Farage, 25 March 2014
(Debate in *The Guardian*)[7]

"Boris (Johnson) negotiated in Europe. I seem to remember last time he did a deal with the Germans, he came back with three nearly-new water cannon."

— Theresa May, 30 June 2016
(Press launch of her Conservative Party Leadership bid)

---

[7] Nick Clegg v Nigel Farage: the tale of the tape (25/03/2014, The Guardian - https://goo.gl/sszlJb)

THE INEXORABLE RISE OF POPULISM IN FRANCE.

- **Country:** France

- **Eligible to vote:** 46,083,260 (2012)

- **Next Presidential election:** 23 April 2017

- **GDP:** $2.42 trillion (2015 est.)

- **Public debt:** 96.2% of GDP (2015 est.)

- **Unemployment:** 10.2% (2015)

- **Population below poverty line:** 8.1% (2012 est.)

- **Inflation rate:** 0.1% (2015 est.)

(Source: The CIA World Factbook[8] & Eurostat[9])

KEY NAMES:

- **Jean-Luc Mélenchon,** MEP, leader of the *Front de Gauche*, a far-left political party.

---

[8] The World Factbook - France (Central Intelligence Agency - https://goo.gl/jV1epw)
[9] Government deficit/surplus, debt and associated data (Eurostat - https://goo.gl/g5da98)

- **Nicolas Sarkozy**, former President and former leader of *Les Républicains*, a right-wing political party.

- **Marine Le Pen**, MEP, leader of the *Front National*, a far-right political party.

First stop in our exclusive reporting on the way populism has been spreading so far in Europe, in the US and in Latin America in recent years. Our journey starts in France.

How does France compare to Britain as regard to populism? How can we explain the recent rise of populism and extremism in France, and what connects them?

First, you must look at what has caused the rise of the populist vote in the world's fifth largest economy: Heavy unemployment (unemployment rate in France: 10.2 per cent, youth unemployment rate: 23.3 per cent, according to *INSEE France*)[10], fears over immigration and terrorism, unsettled social issues and political scandals and corruption.

When the lid of the Populism-in-the-box pops open in France, three names pop out of the box: Jean-Luc Mélenchon, Nicolas Sarkozy and Marine Le Pen.

---

[10] France Unemployment Rate 1996-2016 (19/05/2016, INSEE France - http://goo.gl/jMHHSn)

Jean-Luc Mélenchon.

Jean-Luc Mélenchon is a hard left-wing MEP and former Socialist Party minister who has been very loud and critical about President Sarkozy's policies since 2008 when he left the Socialists and created his own party, the *Front de Gauche* – a rather odd mix of disappointed socialists, Trotskyists, communists, revolutionaries, and anti-capitalists. After he managed to get a surprising 11 per cent of the votes at the 2012 Presidential election that saw Nicolas Sarkozy losing to François Hollande, Mélenchon didn't stop arguing. Whether the new president was issued from the left or not, he kept on criticising the new resident at the Elysée Palace and the new policies he disagreed with.

Mélenchon's fight for his principles, regardless of who the president is, certainly has something of honour. However, some sharp differences started to appear in the way his party's leaders wanted to lead the far-left party.

Mélenchon's enormous ego – rather than his great principles – got in the way. From a man on a mission when he left the Socialist Party, he slowly turned into a childish attention-seeker who simply craved media attention, seeking to be interviewed everywhere and appearing everywhere a camera was broadcasting, even on entertainment TV programmes, or in the street with only a few protesters behind him.

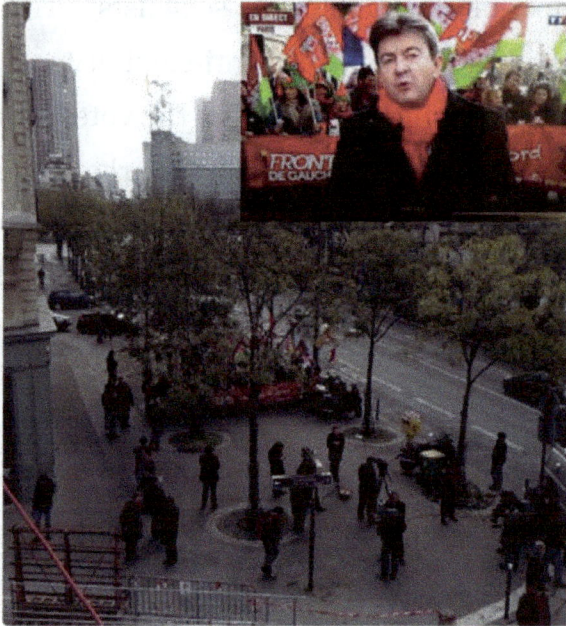

Mathieu Baudier
@mbaudier

Mise en scène médiatique de @JLMelenchon ?
La foule du Front de Gauche à la télé et... en
vrai. via @stefandevries

View translation

12:16 PM - 1 Dec 2013

Yet, in 2015, Mélenchon announced his candidacy for the
2017 Presidential election with a populist manifesto based on
Euroscepticism, a new French Constitution, full wealth sharing
and environmental planning, among other topics. In May 2016,
his campaign website had received over 100,000 individual

support signatures.[11] However, for many of his party's supporters and voters, his constant attention-seeking attitude now means that the man has failed to capture the people's hopes and materialise a real political change in the country.

It was indeed Mélenchon's credibility – or rather what was left of it – that made the leaders of the *Parti Communiste* (PC) vote against supporting him in his new Presidential endeavour.[12] *"Unfortunately, I think a part of the communists are fed up with the type of words used by Jean-Luc Mélenchon sometimes to talk about us"*, party Senator Pierre-Laurent explained – a few days earlier, Mélenchon had been reported having called the communists *"idiots"*. *"They also have the feeling that instead of helping us to unite the Left, Jean-Luc slows us down."*

Mélenchon was angry that some communist leaders had mentioned the possibility of forming a coalition with former minister Arnaud Montebourg and said about it that: *"If their official policy is 'Anyone but Mélenchon', they will soon find themselves eating stones instead of fresh bread."*

The communists' refusal to support him means that Mélenchon will now struggle to get the required 500 signatures

---

[11] Fort de 100.000 soutiens, Mélenchon veut "enraciner" son programme dans les esprits (01/05/2016, PublicSenat.fr - http://goo.gl/lvZKdi)
[12] Pour Pierre Laurent, Mélenchon "exaspère" une partie des communistes (06/11/2016, L'Express - https://goo.gl/WSk2MH)

to be a candidate in the 2017 Presidential election.

Whether Mélenchon manages to be a candidate or whether he gets any support at all from small radical parties, his mere presence on the ballot paper will be dwarfed by the multiplication of candidacy on the Left of the Socialist Party, leaving a wide gap in the electorate to two other individuals: a former president, Nicolas Sarkozy, and a woman on the opposite side of the political spectrum, Marine Le Pen.

Nicolas Sarkozy.

Nicolas Sarkozy is a right-wing politician who was President of France between 2007-2012, before being defeated by François Hollande in 2012. After his defeat, he vowed to retire from public life. Not for very long, however. First, Sarkozy came back to politics in September 2014 in order to take back control of his political party, before launching a bid to become his party's candidate for the 2017 Presidential elections.

As a president, Sarkozy's style was quite controversial from the start. One of his first decisions after being elected was to give himself a substantial pay rise to match his European counterparts: from £100,000 per year to £171,000 per year.[13]

---

[13] Sarkozy demands 140 per cent increase in pay (31/10/2007, The Telegraph -

He also created a controversial "Ministry of Immigration, Integration, National Identity and Co-Development".

Super obsessed with his image, his look and his wife/top model/singer's portrayal in the media, Sarkozy was also a control-freak president whom some French media nicknamed "Hyper-president" after his election to describe his desire to control everything, including taking control over decisions and responsibilities that usually lie with the Prime Minister, not the President, such as domestic policies.

There was, however, something one would call the "Sarkozy paradox". It was the way Nicolas Sarkozy, who has always appeared so much in control of everything, from government policies to media censorship/bias to his own image or his wife's, could easily lose absolute control of himself on occasions and use such inappropriate language that one could think he either needed to take some anger management courses or should get a better team to advise him on his outbursts. As Interior Minister, he, for instance, called young criminals in Paris suburbs' projects *"voyous"* (thugs) and *"racaille"* (scum) in 2005. When visiting the 2008 Paris International Agriculture Fair, as a man refused to shake his hand, Sarkozy – president at the time – answered with a, *"Casse-toi alors, pauv'con, va!" ("Get lost, then, you poor dumb-ass!")*

---

https://goo.gl/VbGfvD)

Were these simply PR provocations or the proof of a real impulsive personality? Populist politicians are usually very talented at crossing the line when deemed necessary, i.e. when they know it will benefit them and raise their profile. For them, there is no such a thing as bad publicity. Indeed, Nicolas Sarkozy isn't afraid to insult a member of the general public in front of the cameras because he knows his supporters and aides will find all sorts of reasons to justify the outburst. The same thing happened with Donald Trump insulting Muslims, Mexicans, women, calling his Democrat rival "Crooked Hillary" or getting even very personal at times during his campaign for the US Presidency.

Another "populist" talent of Nicolas Sarkozy's seemed to be his ability to say one thing in the morning and its complete opposite by the end of the day. When he was a candidate for the 2007 Presidential election, Sarkozy happily signed the *"Pacte écologique"* (an environmental charter with objectives and propositions the new president would agree to apply as part of his governmental policies to prevent the destruction of our planet) of renowned French environmentalist Nicolas Hulot. Quite naturally, a couple of months after his election, Nicolas Sarkozy indeed launched the *"Grenelle de l'environnement"*, a cross-party round table with the aim to define the key points of public policy on ecological and sustainable development issues by the end of the president's mandate, in 2012. In a speech he gave to his supporters in 2009, he even claimed that, to him, ecology was *"not an ideology, not some whim, not a thing, not a strategy, not a political positioning. It's a conviction."*[14] Seven years on, what was left of Sarkozy's conviction during his campaign to win his party's nomination? He totally turned his back on it.

Speaking before businessmen in a private event on 14 September 2016, he was reported by French weekly *Marianne* to have said: *"The climate has been changing for the last 4 billion years. The Sahara has not become a desert because of industries. Only the arrogant man can believe that we have changed the climate."*[15] In less than 10 years, Sarkozy's "conviction" as an ecology lover turned into the rhetoric of a climate-change denier oddly similar to Donald Trump's climate-change claims. Remember? *"NBC News just called it the great freeze — coldest weather in years. Is our country still spending money on the GLOBAL WARMING HOAX?"*[16]

Another example of Nicolas Sarkozy's "World of Contradictions" was on the subject of Islam. In Riyadh, Saudi Arabia, on 14 January 2008, the then-president called Islam *"one of the greatest and most beautiful civilisations the world*

---

[14] Régionales : Nicolas Sarkozy prône l'« ouverture » à l'écologie (30/11/2009, Les Echos - https://goo.gl/sqLWjH)

[15] L'hallucinant virage climato-sceptique de Nicolas Sarkozy (14/09/2016, Marianne - https://goo.gl/Q0S81y)

[16] Yes, Donald Trump did call climate change a Chinese hoax (03/06/2016, PoliticalFact.com - https://goo.gl/hAQuIM)

has known".[17] Two years later, he imposed a controversial ban on the wearing of the burka in public. In June 2016, he asked a hall of his party's MPs: *"In the years ahead what will be left of France?"* He then went on calling on people to *"wake up"* to defend the French national identity and claimed that France was a *"Christian country"* that must be *"respected ... by those who wish to live in it"*, i.e. openly referring to his new favourite campaign target: Muslim migrants.[18] Another day, Sarkozy called for a nationwide ban of the burkini *"to preserve public order"*[19] and, in the same speech given in August 2016 to launch his 2017 bid, he added: *"Where is the authority when it is the minorities who govern? Our identity is under threat when we accept an immigration policy that makes no sense."*[20] Finally, in a book released in August 2016, *Tout pour la France* (Everything for France), Sarkozy wrote: *"Let's say it clearly without any polemic, it's not with religions that the Republic has difficulties today, but with one of them that has not done the work, necessary as well as inevitable, to integrate"*.

Why do all these hypocritical contradictions and populist

---

[17] Sarkozy sparks French debate over God and faith (17/01/2008, Reuters UK - https://goo.gl/8pPJYy)

[18] Sarkozy clashes with presidential rival Juppé over Islam in France (13/06/29016, RFI - https://goo.gl/K6INOY)

[19] Nicolas Sarkozy veut "une loi d'interdiction" du Burkini (25/08/2016, iTele - https://goo.gl/qPUC1N)

[20] Sarkozy on immigration and the burkini ban - Video (26/08/2016, Channel 4 News - https://goo.gl/sRy3kM)

promises even matter? Because Nicolas Sarkozy is the example of an opportunist politician turned populist for the sake of being elected. The more controversial, the more votes, the better. So he thought... Until, in a rather humiliating election, he failed to qualify for the second round of his party's primaries in November 2016.[21] If it was not humiliating enough, it is Sarkozy's former prime minister, François Fillon, who was elected candidate for the centre-right.

In order to achieve his ambition to become President of France for the second time – a revenge he so wanted to take on President Hollande who defeated him in 2012 and who decided not to run in 2017 anyway – Sarkozy had decided to shamelessly copy Marine Le Pen's extremist and populist promises and Donald Trump's outrageous speeches. The latter could somehow (but not only!) be explained by the fact that, according to French weekly *L'Obs*, *"Nicolas Sarkozy has always dreamed of becoming President of the United States. It's all about fulfilling his father's dream"*.[22]

Analysing him today matters. Indeed, he should be regarded as the typical example of an opportunistic character who managed his way to the top thanks to his populist stance.

---

[21] Sarkozy defeated in primary for French right's presidential candidate (20/11/2016 - The Guardian - https://goo.gl/r6WrJM)
[22] Primaire à droite : comment Sarkozy imite Trump (17/09/2016, L'Obs - https://goo.gl/kHxpfl)

Scandal-ridden Nicolas Sarkozy already had a go at the French presidency (2007-2012) with an arrogant and ostentatious attitude most French people despised and still remember very well. His attitude during the primary campaign, obviously, raised some serious questions once again about his ability to tell the truth or just fantasise about a supposedly lost French way of life that never existed only to create tensions between communities and between people, while himself living in a comfy and protected bubble at the Elysée Palace when/if he was to become president.

In what was seen to be his must-win centre-right primary nomination for the 2017 Presidential election, Nicolas Sarkozy was not exactly sparing with his criticisms of his main rival, former prime minister Alain Juppé, whilst leaving some breathing space to another rival, his former PM François Fillon and overlooking his power of disturbance.[23]

Juppé was a softer unifying conservative figure in *Les Républicains*. The Mayor of Bordeaux, who was once the most unpopular French PM during President Chirac's first mandate, advocated for more tolerance towards religion, immigration and stood in the primaries with, more generally, a far less divisive approach than Sarkozy's, to bring people and

---

[23] Les Républicains primary: The runners and riders as the French centre-right selects its presidential candidate (16/09/2016, EUROPP LSE Blog – https://goo.gl/eAbV6d)

communities together instead of endlessly blaming them and hypocritically finger-pointing and, especially so, stigmatising Muslims in France. (Contrary to popular belief, Muslims represent only 5.6 per cent of the population in France, i.e. 3-4 million, according to a report published on 18 September 2016 by independent think-tank *Institut Montaigne.*)[24]

In the end, 66.5 per cent of the electorate of the centre-right chose the middle-man: a fervent Roman Catholic Fillon and a fan of Margaret Thatcher. A man who said that *"France is more right-wing than it has ever been"*, wants to *"restore France's pride and institutions"*, calls France *"a nation that deserves better"* and is absolutely a right-wing conservative politician who believes in the *"French values"*. He also said of Socialist François Hollande's presidency that it had been *"pathetic"*.

The recent terror attacks in France, the endless rise of far-right Marine Le Pen in the polls and the controversy around the burkini, had pushed Nicolas Sarkozy to step up his hard-line rhetoric and add fuel to the fire on a nearly daily basis. From calling for the *Le Touquet agreement* to be scrapped (to get rid of the so-called Jungle in Calais, so that Britain controls its border in Dover and no longer in Calais – an agreement Sarkozy himself signed as president!), to calling for *"Every Frenchman suspected of being linked to terrorism to be placed*

24 Un islam français est possible (18/09/2016, Institut Montaigne - https://goo.gl/8uJS0r)

in a detention centre",[25] promising to end mass immigration, promising to end communitarianism, taking a tough stance on law and order, reasserting the French cultural and religious identity, shouting that schools should stop offering non-pork options at lunch, the former president has copy-pasted much of Le Pen's major policies.

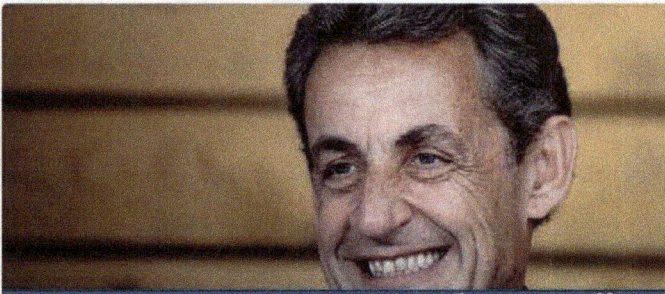

Steve Rose
@steveplrose

If elected, Sarkozy would prevent Muslim and Jewish students from accessing non-pork meals in schools

theguardian

Nicolas Sarkozy declares candidacy for French presidential election
Former leader says key issue for France is 'how to defend our lifestyle without cutting ourselves off from the world'
theguardian.com

"If you want to become French, you speak French, you live like the French. We will no longer settle for integration that does not work, we will require assimilation. Once you become

[25] Sarkozy sur le terrorisme : "Notre riposte doit changer de dimension" (11/09/2016, Le Journal du Dimanche – https://goo.gl/0cKCxT)

French, your ancestors are the Gauls. [sic] *'I love France, I learned the history of France, I see myself as French' is what you must say,"* Sarkozy also said, blaming out loud the so-called *"tyranny of minorities"* and claiming to be *"the voice of the silent majority"*. What better way to create discord and intolerance through the people's ignorance? Trumpesque!

For information, in his book "De Bello Gallico" (Book I, Chapter I)[26] Julius Caesar himself explained how tribal and diverse the Gauls were, and not a united people from which the French identity could have originated from: *"All Gaul is divided into three parts, one of which the Belgae inhabit, the Aquitani another, those who in their own language are called Celts, in ours Gauls, the third. All these differ from each other in language, customs and laws."*

In a quite ironic twist, though, Marine Le Pen herself absolutely objected to Sarkozy's sudden adoption of her extremist policies and "values", and didn't hesitate to speak out loud about it. She knew the man didn't actually share her or her party's extremist convictions and was mostly working the cameras to please her supporters, her electorate. It was second nature to him. So, the populist Le Pen portrayed Sarkozy as... a populist: *"At every election, Nicolas Sarkozy shows himself as*

---

[26] The Project Gutenberg EBook of "De Bello Gallico" and Other Commentaries by Caius Julius Caesar" (Gutemberg.org - https://goo.gl/azEsjI)

someone tough, with authority on immigration. The truth is that every time he has been in power, whether as the interior minister or as president, he has been the sponsor of a massive wave of immigration, a total laxity, a devastating communitarianism, a positive discrimination that goes against the values of the French Republic, the collapse of police resources and the refusal to respect the voice of the people."[27]

Sarkozy's position was to fight at all costs to have a chance to appear on the ballot papers at the first round of the Presidential election in 2017, whereas, as far as she is concerned – and because all the opinion polls already showed that she would easily qualify for the second round – Marine Le Pen had only one thing in mind: find the magic formula that would make her win the second round of the Presidential election, whoever her opponent was then.

Immigration was not Nicolas Sarkozy's only interest though. On Tuesday 27 September 2016, he announced that, if elected president of France in May 2017, he would give Britain a chance to reverse the Brexit vote, raising eyebrows across the European Union. Could such a decision, democratically taken by the people of a sovereign member state of the EU, be

---

[27] Présidentielle : Marine Le Pen tacle Sarkozy, «promoteur d'une immigration massive» (17/09/2016, Le Parisien – https://goo.gl/gmjhV7)

overlooked? What was in it for Sarkozy?

The right-wing politician had spoken to 500 business leaders at the *"Primaires de l'Économie"*, in Paris.[28] A forum organised by five associations of start-ups, investors, and business leaders,[29] where five other candidates to the primaries of the right-wing party *Les Républicains* had also been invited to pitch for 12 minutes each about their economic, tax and social plans, before facing a Q&A.[30] The former president, who then only used three minutes of the twelve allocated, explained that his big plan to save the European Union was to negotiate a new treaty with Germany that could persuade Great Britain not to leave.

Excusez-moi? (I beg your pardon?) How dare a French politician, a candidate for the French presidency, tell us Brits that we should not leave the European Union when a majority of us voted to Leave? Shocking!

Tea?

Well. The offer was interesting, to say the least. If Prime Minister Theresa May was seeking a way out of the EU referendum result, a way to get out of the Brexit trap, a way to

---

[28] Les Primaires de l'Economie (27/09/2016, FrenchWeb.fr - https://goo.gl/Kq9hKv)

[29] Twitter - @Chef_entreprise (28/09/2016, Chef d'Entreprise - https://goo.gl/v5uxBs)

[30] Présidentielle 2017 : les candidats à la primaire de droite passent leur grand oral de l'économie (27/09/2016, La Tribune - https://goo.gl/ZZ1eDK)

keep Britain in, she might well have found one with Nicolas Sarkozy's offer.

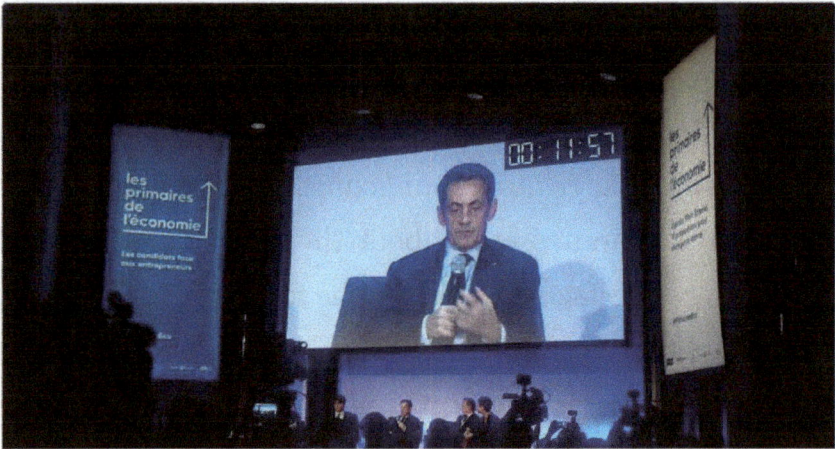

Chef d'Entreprise
@Chef_entreprise

"Diminuer la dépense publique et les impôts" c'est le leitmotiv de @NicolasSarkozy #PrimairesEco

5:02 PM - 27 Sep 2016

What Sarkozy was in fact showing was a long-term vision of what a modern and refreshed European Union could look like. Sure, it was HIS vision only, but so far, no other European leader or politician had come with anything new to offer to make the EU work. On the contrary, all the discussions and speeches from all sides of the political spectrum had been full of the same old rhetoric: *"We must change the EU"*, *"We must reform the EU"*, *"We need a new project"*, *"Brexit must be a wake-up call for us all"*, etc. The only alternative voices and comments heard since the EU referendum result had come from nationalists and far-right political parties across Europe, the likes of Nigel Farage, UKIP, and Marine Le Pen, claiming victory and wishing for only one thing: the end of the European Union as soon as possible – a thought certainly shared by their Russian friend, Vladimir Putin.

If three months after the British EU referendum result *"Brexit means Brexit"* still meant nothing in London, it was regrettable to see that Brexit meant *"the same old Europe"* in the 27 other European capitals. No one had come with a plan to move the EU forward. No one, but Nicolas Sarkozy.

During the summer, the former president himself seemed to have been on a long journey to elaborate his own vision of what the EU without, or with, Britain should look like. A few hours after the Brexit result, for example, he had given an interview to the French weekly *Journal du Dimanche* in which he explained how he had expected the Brexit win because of the general *"lack of* [European] *common strategies for growth and employment, the lack of Schengen reforms and the lack of answers on immigration policies"*, before adding: *"If I were president, I would offer to Germany to create a five-point project to submit to the other European leaders with no intervention from the Brussels technocracy"*.[31] He then later

---

[31] Nicolas Sarkozy : "Je m'attendais au Brexit" (27/06/2016, Le Journal du Dimanche -

talked about Hollande and Merkel's inability to deal with Brexit and how the British government would take all its time to leave the EU. *"Expect 10 horrible months until the French election"*, he even said at a weekly gathering of his party's MPs.[32] He also talked about Brexit as *"a great economic opportunity"*, a great time to steal the spotlight from the British. He said that it was time *"to make Paris the start-ups hub"*, i.e. instead of London.[33]

To the business leaders he had explained that if elected, he would have flown to Berlin to meet with German Chancellor Angela Merkel to work with her on a draft of a new EU treaty, and the following day he would have travelled to London. Sarkozy was then reported by the *Financial Times* as having said: *"I would tell the British, you've gone out, but we have a new treaty on the table so you have an opportunity to vote again. But this time not on the old Europe, on the new Europe. Do you want to stay? If yes, so much the better. Because I can't accept losing Europe's second-largest economy while we are negotiating with Turkey over its EU membership. And if it's no, then it's a real no. You're in or you're out."*[34]

The very fact that Nicolas Sarkozy had come with a plan –

---

https://goo.gl/d3kxts)

[32] Brexit: "10 mois horribles" selon Sarkozy (28/06/2016, Le Figaro - https://goo.gl/7tlKLE)

[33] Twitter – @NicolasSarkozy (27/09/2016, Nicolas Sarkozy - https://goo.gl/yQVjnc)

[34] Sarkozy vows to offer UK exit from Brexit if he wins French poll (27/09/2016, Financial Times - https://goo.gl/xYVZo7)

a rare thing for politicians nowadays, it seems – that would modernise and make the European Union more relevant, and that could also accommodate Britain to the point it could eventually decide to stay in the EU, was an important occurrence. Again, he was the first and only major European figure to have come with a plan!

What was in it for Sarkozy? Threatened by endless scandals in France, the release of a controversial book by one of his former advisors and by newly uncovered documents allegedly showing that he received 6.5 million euros from former Libyan leader Gaddafi to finance his campaign for the presidency in 2007,[35] would Nicolas Sarkozy have been using the EU and Brexit as a diversion? Very unlikely. The announcement would certainly not have had any major effect on his campaign.

By somehow "informally" mentioning the Brexit situation to an audience of entrepreneurs rather than publicly, Nicolas Sarkozy was not really trying to appeal to the French voters. Sarkozy's vision for the EU has been almost unreported in the French media. There was a reason for that: the French were far less interested in the British exit from the EU than in the issues of immigration, the fight against terrorism or the recent increase in the unemployment rate.

---

[35] Un carnet consignait en 2007 les millions libyens de Nicolas Sarkozy (27/09/2016, Mediapart - https://goo.gl/LLJLHi)

While it certainly was a flop in France, it was not so abroad, especially in Britain, where the Financial Times first reported the news. One could have accused Sarkozy of trying to woo the French expats living in Britain, who mostly voted for Francois Hollande in 2012 (53 per cent of the vote). They rightly were worried about the Brexit situation in which the British Government seemed to be prepared to use them and all the other EU citizens living in the UK as a bargaining chip during the Brexit trade negotiations. The French expats could have been the kingmakers during the May 2017 election. It was therefore likely a part of Sarkozy's thinking to indirectly tell them: *"I'm thinking of you. I want to help you. I will secure your stay in the UK. Vote for me!"*

It might also be interesting, this time, to look beyond the man's usual populist claims and promises. Indeed, in 2005, when 55 per cent of French voters rejected the Treaty establishing a Constitution for Europe via a referendum decided by the then President Jacques Chirac, the whole of Europe thought it was going to be the end of the EU.[36]

Then, in 2007, Nicolas Sarkozy became president with a pledge to renegotiate and ratify a new treaty without the need for a referendum. The treaty was to be known as the Treaty of

---

[36] Treaty establishing a Constitution for Europe (16/12/2004, Official Journal of the European Union - https://goo.gl/hMkuhg)

Lisbon, which still governs the way the EU works today.[37] In February 2008, the treaty was voted for by the French Parliament and ratified.

In Ireland, however, a referendum took place in June 2008 and 53.4 per cent of the voters chose to reject the new treaty. After 16 months of work and negotiations with the rest of the EU countries, Ireland held a second referendum on the same treaty and finally 67.1 per cent of the voters accepted it.

It is worth reflecting on the possibility that, as for the French and Irish referendums just mentioned, if Nicolas Sarkozy – free from any political duty in France since his elimination for the 2017 election, was to create a new treaty that could satisfy the British government enough that it would decide to hold a new referendum to decide on whether Britain would remain in the new EU or leave for good and if the British people were then convinced that that new treaty would benefit the UK, Brexit would just not happen at all.

Nicolas Sarkozy would then be hailed a hero across Europe for saving the EU28, a strategic genius. The power of decision in the new EU would not be the usual French-German couple any longer, but a French-British-German trio. Theresa May would be regarded as the woman who saved the honour of

---

Britain in face of expected Brexit chaos and would easily win the General Elections in 2020 (or before) with the larger majority in history in the House of Commons. As for Nicolas Sarkozy, he could run for president of the European Council after Donald Tusk's mandate ends either in May 2017 or in December 2019 with the treaty that kept the EU28 together in his pocket and win – thus fulfilling somehow his father's impossible dream of having a son who is president of the United States of America.

All this is pure politics fiction anyway: François Fillon won the centre-right primary and he is now their candidate for the 2017 election in France. As for Nicolas Sarkozy becoming President of the European Council in 2017 or 2019, let's say that it currently looks less like reality and more like science fiction. But who knows? Everything seems to be possible nowadays: Brexit, Trump...

A final word about Nicolas Sarkozy and his odd relationship with Vladimir Putin. A documentary on the rise of Vladimir Putin to power recently screened on French TV claims to have shed new lights on the odd start in the relationship between former French President Nicolas Sarkozy and his Russian counterpart. The documentary screened on French public channel *France 2*, *"Le Mystère Poutine"* (*The Putin Mystery*) may have shed new lights on what happened in 2007 at the G8 Summit in Heiligendamm, Germany, when Nicolas

Sarkozy, who had just recently been elected president of France, appeared at a press conference breathless, which some journalists thought might have been caused by some heavy alcohol consumption with the Russian president.[38]

In the documentary, however, a well-known French journalist who was held hostage by Daesh in Syria for 10 months and who wrote a book on Putin's networks in France (*"La France russe : Enquête sur les réseaux de Poutine"*),[39] Nicolas Hénin, explains that Sarkozy was absolutely not drunk, but KO.[40]

Hénin goes on to describe a private meeting between Nicolas Sarkozy and Vladimir Putin that took place before Sarkozy's Press conference, and that has been reported to him, in which the then French president is said to have had a cowboy attitude at first towards his Russian counterpart, telling him that from now on, *"there will be no more taboo. The hundreds of dead in Chechnya, it's unacceptable. The Russian journalist Anna Politkovskaya who has been assassinated, this too is unacceptable..."*

The journalist explains that Putin, after having remained silent the whole time, kept quiet a bit longer when Sarkozy had finished talking and only stared at him.

---

[38] Sarkozy Drunk ? (07/06/2007, YouTube - https://youtu.be/g1HCFHjLndQ)

[39] La France russe : Enquête sur les réseaux de Poutine (Amazon - https://goo.gl/ktLVQ1)

[40] Le mystère Poutine (15/12/2016, YouTube - https://youtu.be/cml2bsWz1tQ)

He then opened his mouth to ask: *"Are you done, now?"* As Sarkozy answered *"Yes,"* Putin is said to have launched his verbal counter-attack: *"I am going to explain this to you... See the size of your country?... See the size of my country?... Either you continue to talk to me with that tone of voice and I smash you to pieces... Or you calm down and you will see, as you just became president of France, I can make you the King of Europe!"*

According to Nicolas Hénin, the reason why a few minutes later Nicolas Sarkozy appeared so shaken at his G8 Press conference was not because he was drunk, but rather because he had been verbally and morally knocked-out by the Russian president.

On that day, something definitely happened for Sarkozy suddenly became a fervent supporter of Putin. His support has never faded since...[41]

If Nicolas Hénin's claims are true (this is quite difficult to prove, unless one of the protagonists confirms them or if someone possesses an audio or video of the scene) and that Vladimir Putin has indeed threatened and bullied the newly elected president of the fifth world power, one can only imagine how the Russian president may behave with leaders of smaller

---

[41] How Nicolas Sarkozy Went From Fierce Putin Critic To Ardent Admirer (19/11/2016, Buzzfeed - https://goo.gl/0MZJqn)

nations in order to get what he wants for Russia and turn them into allies against their nation's own interests.

Marine Le Pen.

Marine Le Pen is the daughter of far-right politician Jean-Marie Le Pen who, between the 1980s and the 2010s, gradually saw his xenophobic party, the *Front National*, growing in supporters and in voters to eventually reach the second round of the Presidential election in 2002 – only to be beaten by the conservative Jacques Chirac,[42] thanks to a remarkable republican front that called voters from the left to the right wings of the political spectrum to vote to defeat Le Pen at all costs. Chirac won 82 per cent of the votes to Le Pen's 18 per cent – the largest ever win in a French presidential election.

As Le Pen senior eventually handed over the reins of his party to his daughter Marine Le Pen, in 2011, she obviously kept hammering the same Eurosceptic, anti-establishment, and anti-immigration message as her father before her for a while, but with a difference: she made sure she was keeping a certain distance with her father's openly racist and xenophobic comments, keeping skinheads and neo-Nazi groups out of the

---

[42] Jacques Chirac, profile (Encyclopædia Britannica - https://www.britannica.com/biography/Jacques-Chirac)

party, etc. Marine Le Pen's "detoxification" of the *Front National* had one aim: making her name and her party look respectable enough even to people who had never voted for her father before and who would never vote for her party otherwise: voters from the centre and the left.

Le Pen's major policies to be elected president, i.e. Her list of big ideas "to save France" – which Nicolas Sarkozy shamelessly kept picking ideas from – haven't much changed over the years: the protection of the French economy from "unfair" competition and globalisation, giving priority to French citizens in jobs and housing, the end to mass immigration, taking a tough stance on law and order issues, reasserting the French cultural identity and being a strong and independent France in defence and foreign affairs, the withdrawing from the Euro and the promise to organise a referendum on EU membership to get France out of the EU, the "Frexit". Empty promises and extremist views that may well take her to the French Presidency in 2017 with the precious help of Nicolas Sarkozy who unconsciously, or not, made Marine Le Pen's extreme views and policies increasingly mainstream, increasingly acceptable to the French.

After the attack in Nice, on 14 July 2016, and months of growing anger towards the authorities in the country, the leader of the Front National, who is never the last to link the free movement of people in Europe to the rise of terror – even if this is yet to be proven – predictably called for the resignation of the interior minister because of the mounting death toll from terror attacks in recent years in France. *"In any other country in the world, a minister with a toll as horrendous as Bernard Cazeneuve – 250 dead in 18 months – would have quit,"* she said. *"With such a crisis, we must say: Hollande* [President], *Valls* [Prime Minister], *Cazeneuve* [Interior Minister], *Sarkozy* [former President] *and co., never ever again, never ever THEM again!"*

When Prime Minister Manuel Valls awkwardly said on TV that *"France will have to learn to live with terrorism"*,[43] it sounded for many like a terrible admission of powerlessness to control the situation or give oneself the right tools to fight terrorism. That admission was light years away from what people really wanted to hear from their government after such atrocity.

The French people's deep sadness after the repeated terrorist attacks has now turned into anger at who they see as clueless and powerless leaders. After the migrant crisis, the terrorist threat in France has become yet another if not THE main reason that makes Marine Le Pen a clear favourite to win the 2017 Presidential election, even though her solutions to

---

treat the problem are as divisive as her words, or her own niece's, Marion Maréchal-Le Pen – one of the youngest MPs in France, who disturbingly told the party supporters after the Nice attack: *"Either we kill Islamism or it will kill us again and again. You are with us and against Islamism, or you are against us and for Islamism... Those who choose the status quo become complicit with our enemies."*

CNN International ✓
@cnni

🐦 Follow

French far right leader Marine Le Pen calls for "a real war" to end Islamic fundamentalism cnn.it/29K9hoJ

3:44 PM - 16 Jul 2016

↩ 🔁 156 ♥ 142

After her grandfather and her aunt, Marion Maréchal-Le Pen is the third generation of what should be seen as a dangerous far-right dynastic populism that is exponentially rising in France and standing now, more than ever, on the doorstep of power.

In the future, her niece – who is a hardcore conservative in the far-right party – could maybe even be a danger for Marine Le Pen herself, if she is to fail to be elected president...

"Et tu, Brute?"

Conclusion.

The combination of the continued stigmatisation of the Muslim community with the endless finger-pointing at Middle Eastern refugees and the blaming of all migrants in general – the scapegoats for the society's ills – by populist politicians such as Sarkozy or Le Pen is dangerously putting France on the verge of a civil war, which could easily be sparked by anything that would be the last drop to add to the rising anger and general exasperation that already reign in France since the terrorist attacks of 13 November 2015 in Paris. (An abominable terrorist attack somewhere on the scale of 9/11, for instance, or something unfortunately as horrible.)

In April 2017, French people will have a choice between unleashing once and for all their old demons – filled with hate and a deep desire for destruction – at their own peril by electing Marine Le Pen, or believe a second-class déjà vu former prime minister and his windy and divisive promises or... calm down a moment, get their act together and vote with their heads without impulsiveness for a candidate who will bring them hope not fear, togetherness not discord, understanding not intolerance, dexterity not ignorance, competency not ineptness, authority not extremism. Is there anyone matching that description in France?

In an interview he gave to *Europe 1* radio on the day Donald Trump was elected President in the United States, former French Prime Minister Jean-Pierre Raffarin said: *"Since Brexit, the front line of reason no longer exists. It means that the main news for the French people is that Marine Le Pen can win in France."* He also said that in his opinion it meant that *"extreme populism can win and that Ms Le Pen, with simple answers, can win in France."*[44]

Populism in France is neither a left-wing nor a right-wing ideology. It has wrongly been used by politicians as a strategy to win votes. It has, instead, allowed nationalism and extremism to grow into a dangerous weed that now threatens to take over the entire garden of the republic. Only a genuine message of hope may still kill that weed, before it is too late.

* * *

---

[44] Victoire de Trump : "Ça veut dire que Marine Le Pen peut gagner", selon Raffarin (09/11/2016, Europe 1 - https://goo.gl/tcxHdn)

"Immigration is an organised replacement of our population.
This threatens our very survival.
We don't have the means to integrate
those who are already here.
The result is endless cultural conflict."

— Marine Le Pen, 27 April 2011
(Interview to *RT*)[45]

---

[45] I want to free France from EU straitjacket – far-right party leader (27/04/2011, RT - http://on.rt.com/sux6fh)

THE PARTY FOR FREEDOM THAT WANTS TO RESTRICT FREEDOM IN HOLLAND.

- **Country:** The Netherlands

- **Eligible to vote:** 12,689,810 (2012)

- **Next general election:** 15 March 2017

- **GDP:** $750.7 billion (2015 est.)

- **Public debt:** 65.3% of GDP (2015 est.)

- **Unemployment:** 7% (2015)

- **Population below poverty line:** 9.1% (2013 est.)

- **Inflation rate:** 0.2% (2015 est.)

(Source: The CIA World Factbook[46] & Eurostat[47])

KEY INDIVIDUALS:

---

[46] The World Factbook - Greece (Central Intelligence Agency - https://goo.gl/pVYuqI)
[47] Unemployment by sex and age - monthly average (Eurostat - https://goo.gl/tdwoLC)

- **Party for Freedom** (*Partij voor de Vrijheid*, **PVV**), far-right populist and nationalist party.

- **Geert Wilders,** far-right politician and more generally Islam hater, leader of the Party for Freedom.

The Party for Freedom originally started in 2004 as a one-man party, with Geert Wilders sitting on his own in the Dutch parliament after having been sacked from the conservative-liberal People's Party for Freedom and Democracy (*Volkspartij voor Vrijheid en Democratie*, VVD) because of the way he was challenging the party line in public statements whilst being the VVD's public spokesman, especially with his outspoken criticism of Islam and his opposition to the party's support for Turkey's accession to the EU.

Turkey's accession to the EU has been the favourite subject of conversation of many right-wing populists and far- right nationalists during the last decade. One can remember the most recent of such examples: the British referendum on Britain's continuous membership of the European Union (Brexit). The Leave campaigners consciously lied to the electorate and claimed that Turkey was about to become a member of the European, within years, within months, maybe even within days after the result of the referendum. What happened next is history. Nearly 52 per cent of voters chose to listen and believe the alarming populist-in-chiefs Boris, Gove and Farage with the political and economic chaos that came along with it, whilst Turkey is still very far from ready to become a member of the EU (only 1 out of the 35 chapters of the EU-Turkey negotiations has been finalised since October 2005),[48] especially with the failed coup that took place in the summer of 2016 and the crackdown on opposition leaders, journalists, teachers, etc.

In June 2005, when the Dutch voters rejected the EU Constitution with 61.6 per cent of the votes – the EU Constitution that was also rejected by the French a few days earlier in a referendum – Wilders was one of the leading voices for "NO".[49] After the results were announced, he said: *"If you realise that two-thirds of parliament supported the constitution and two out of three people in the land are against, it means a lot is wrong in the country."* It was a first step, a first nationwide win for him. A win that led to more. In the 2006 Dutch general election that followed, the Party for Freedom won 9 seats out of 150 in the parliament.

Geert Wilders has never hidden his long-time ambition. *"I*

---

[48] Accession Negotiations. What is the current status? (Delegation of the European Union to Turkey - https://goo.gl/7nDv5T)
[49] Dutch say 'No' to EU constitution (02/06/2005, BBC News - https://goo.gl/xdtFoI)

want to be Prime Minister," he very confidently said at the end of a party meeting in Venlo, in 2009. *"At some point, it's going to happen and then it will be a big honour to fulfil the post of Prime Minister."*[50]

Wilders had all the reasons in the world to believe he could become the next Prime Minister: the *Party for Freedom* was the most popular in opinion polls with a predicted 21 per cent of the votes in the next general election, which would make it the most powerful party in parliament with 32 seats and get Wilders to fulfil his dream of becoming Prime Minister. The party's sudden popularity was due to the publicity around the prosecution attempts against Wilders – the politician was tried and acquitted for hate speech against Islam in 2011 in a lengthy process, as well as the financial crisis of 2008 that affected everyone.

In the local elections, the Party for Freedom did well: in the town of The Hague, the third largest city in the Netherlands after Amsterdam and Rotterdam, the party finished second (8 seats) behind the *Partij van de Arbeid*, the Dutch Labour party (10 seats). Wilders was ready for the general election of June 2010. Unfortunately for him, although his party did increase its number of seats from 9 to 24, it only received 15.4 per cent of the votes, whilst the socialists and the conservatives had won

---

[50] Wilders: I want to be prime minister (17/03/2009, Dutch News - https://goo.gl/so5q8N)

respectively 30 seats and 31 seats, keeping the Party for Freedom in the third position. With no majority, though, the two major parties had no choice but to form a coalition government, with very controversial parliamentary support from Wilders' party. Wilders was not the prime minister, but he had secured the job of kingmaker.

The coalition lasted nearly two years until Geert Wilders withdrew his support to the government because of new austerity measures it was about to introduce and for which he blamed the European Union. Measures the government didn't waste a minute to remind him that his own party had actually supported earlier on. The end of the coalition led to a new general election in September 2012. After mostly campaigning for the withdrawal of the Netherlands from the EU and for a return to the former Dutch currency, this time, Wilders and his party hit a rock. They lost 9 seats in parliament, ending up with only 15 seats and down to 10.1 per cent of the votes. Worse: the Liberal democrats of Democrats 66 (12 seats) and the Socialist Party (15 seats) were now catching up.

It looked as if Geert Wilders and his Party for Freedom had lost their momentum when again, in March 2014, they suffered more losses in the local elections.

They went into the 2014 European elections with the hope they would change this losing mood into a winning spree.

However, the results weren't good with the Party for Freedom finishing third behind the Christian Democratic Appeal and Democrats 66, reaching only 13.3 per cent of the votes compared to 16.9 per cent in the previous European elections and no new seat gain. Since 2014, however, the popularity of Wilders has sprung mostly through the on-going migrant crisis. The opinion polls have shown a sudden increased interest for his hard stance on immigration, his anti-Islam rhetoric, and his anti-refugee policies. Recently, various opinion polls have even shown his party running neck and neck, slightly in front or slightly behind the VVD, the Prime Minister's party.

In order to energise his supporters and attract more Dutch to vote for him, he recently started to harden his anti-Islam and anti-EU stance and drafted a new manifesto that pledges the closure of every mosque in the Netherlands, a total ban on headscarves in government buildings, a total ban of the Koran, the immediate withdrawal of the EU Schengen open borders agreement and a referendum to get the Netherlands out of the European Union, or "Nexit".[51]

The sudden surge in opinion polls for his party would almost contrast with the dull period up to the local elections of

---

[51] Close all mosques & ban the Koran: Poll-topping Geert Wilders launches 'de-Islamization' manifesto (26/08/2016, RT - https://goo.gl/z6FCSm)

2014 when Wilders' only gain was the international coverage of abusive chants during a party rally in The Hague, where he asked his supporters whether they wanted *"fewer or more Moroccans in your city, and in the Netherlands?" "Fewer, fewer... Moroccans!"* was the answer of the crowd. And a smiling Geert Wilders then told them: *"We're going to organise that!"*

This should not come as a surprise for all along his political career, Wilders has been criticising Islam, calling for the Koran to be banned, opposing the building of new mosques then calling for the closure of all mosques, and calling for the closure of all asylum centres in the Netherlands. From a simple populist character with controversial views, the Dutch have seen him grow into a far-right populist whose portrait can only be matched by Donald Trump. However, on that evening of 2014, he went a step too far. Wilders has since been charged with racial discrimination and inciting hatred.[52]

On 9 December 2016, he was found guilty of inciting discrimination.[53] The court opted not to fine him, arguing the conviction itself was a sufficient punishment for a politician democratically elected. He

---

[52] What Dutch politician Geert Welders' trial says about the far-right in Europe (01/11/2016, Newsweek - https://goo.gl/TqpXbv)
[53] Dutch anti-Islam politician Geert Wilders found guilty in hate speech trial (09/12/2016, The Independent - https://goo.gl/BzWb6Z)

called the trial he did not attend *"political"*, *"a travesty"* and an *"attack on free-speech"*. The Dutch Prime Minister, Mark Rutte, said of his comments that they *"left a bad taste in the mouth"* and that Wilders *"again has gone too far."*

Conclusion.

The "Wilders problem" could easily be summed up with three examples of what the populist politician has recently said.

The first example is an article that he wrote for Dutch daily newspaper *Algemeen Dagblad*, in which he claims that he spoke for *"millions of Dutch people, fed up with the disruption and terror caused by so many Moroccans... If talking about that is an offence, the Netherlands is no longer a free country, but a dictatorship."*[54]

Translation: Wilders is a delusional character who suffers from the Godsend Syndrome. He sees himself as the "voice of the people", whom he only can understand. He is also an ersatz freedom fighter.

The second example is another article that he wrote, this time for alt-right news website *Breitbart*, in which he says: *"I*

[54] Geert Wilders trial throws Netherlands' divisions in sharp relief (31/10/2016, The Guardian - https://goo.gl/MJdguP)

visited Maassluis. It is a town near Rotterdam, where the indigenous Dutch inhabitants have become the victims of immigrant youths of Moroccan descent. [...] Not surprisingly, a poll shows that 43 per cent of the Dutch people want fewer Moroccan immigrants in our country. These people are not racists; they are decent people, patriots who love their country and do not want to lose it."[55]

Translation: According to Wilders, if he develops a blatant prejudice against foreigners, it is because there is prejudice and discrimination against the majority white, indigenous population. Wilders is, in fact, a scaremonger who purposely pits the notion of being an indigenous victim against being a violent immigrant descent. He pits the notion of being a patriotic Dutch against being a foreigner-friendly Dutch. Divide et impera.

The third and final example is a statement that was read out by one of his lawyers during his trial about the 2014 rally in The Hague. *"It is my right and my duty as a politician to speak about the problems in our country,"* he said, claiming that he had done nothing wrong. *"Because the Netherlands has a mega Moroccan problem."*

Translation: Paranoiac Wilders claims that he has never

---

55 Geert Wilders For Breitbart: Let's Lock The Door To Islam (28/10/2016, Breitbart - https://goo.gl/3G0xaY)

done anything wrong, but he is instead the innocent and powerless victim of an obvious political plot to keep him away from the position of power where he could finally save the Netherlands from a gigantic Moroccan threat.

The man who once said: *"Half of Holland loves me and half of Holland hates me. There is no in-between"* is like no other European populist leader. The outspoken politician does accept responsibility for both his racist rants and his xenophobic rhetoric but doesn't consider them as abusive or aggressive, rather a form of his democratic right to freedom of speech.

Wilders believes that saying things like *"Islam is not a religion, it's an ideology, the ideology of a retarded culture"*,[56] *"The Koran is a fascist book which incites violence. That is why this book, just like* Mein Kampf, *must be banned. The book incites hatred and killing and therefore has no place in our* [Dutch] *legal order"*[57] or *"Of course it is a minority that uses the violence, but unfortunately there is a majority of these people who support the idea, and think they are heroes"*[58] has no consequences and they are not hate speeches.

---

[56] 'I don't hate Muslims. I hate Islam,' says Holland's rising political star (17/02/2008, The Guardian - https://goo.gl/n0r3Qn)

[57] In quotes: Geert Wilders (04/10/2010, BBC News - https://goo.gl/7Z0wNo)

[58] The Breitbart Geert Wilders Interview (19/06/2015, Breitbart - https://goo.gl/ZAHgFd)

They definitely are.

Wilders doesn't want to take any responsibility for terrible events that may occur because of his speeches and the hate against Islam and against the foreigners that he spreads all over the Dutch media. When Anders Breivik, the neo-Nazi who carried out the terrifying attacks in Norway in 2011, said that he admired Geert Wilders and his Party for Freedom,[59] Wilders was quick to distance himself from the madman. He didn't want to be associated with him and his terrorism.

In Wilders' opinion, his freedom to talk, insult, abuse and hate, in a sense, should have no limit and he should not be blamed for what he says either. In other words, to Geert Wilders, one man's hate speech is another man's freedom of speech.

In a previous encounter with the Court, in March 2016, the lead prosecutor Wouter Bos told him: *"Freedom of expression is not absolute, it is paired with obligations and responsibilities, the responsibility not to set groups of people against each other."* He added: *"Racism and hatred of foreigners constitute a direct violation of the foundations of*

---

[59] Norway attacks: How far right views created Anders Behring Breivik (30/07/2011, The Guardian - https://goo.gl/YdhNCE)

freedom, democracy and the rule of law."[60]

As Henny Sackers, professor of administrative criminal law at Radboud University in Nijmegen, explained about the hate speech trial, whilst *"the European court says you can criticise religion in public even if it shocks, hurts, or disturbs, in the case of discrimination on grounds of nationality, you can be guilty of an offence in Dutch law if you provoke social unrest. So, I see the chances of a conviction for Wilders as being considerably higher than three years ago."*[61] Though Sackers warned that the trial had come at a very unfortunate time for the Netherlands, as *"whether Wilders is acquitted or convicted, he will present himself as the Dutch Donald Trump, a crusader for the free world. It will always give him a potential electoral advantage."*

Geert Wilders was actually mentioned by US journalist Anne Applebaum in an article published in the Washington Post, in which she wrote about Donald Trump and his relation to the West: *"Geert Wilders, the xenophobic Dutch politician, showed up at the Republican National Convention, where instead of observing, as a Dutch Christian Democrat would*

---

[60] Dutch far-right leader tells court - 'I want fewer Moroccans' (18/03/2016, Reuters - https://goo.gl/osOs7J)

[61] Geert Wilders' trial on inciting hatred charges opens without him (31/10/2016, The Guardian - https://goo.gl/EljnXB)

have done, he agitated on behalf of Trump, too."[62]

Donald Trump, between Nigel Farage, Marine Le Pen, Vladimir Putin, and Geert Wilders, has quite a fan club!

What happens next for the Netherlands is the million-dollar question. By appealing the decision of the judges, Wilders is now able to promote his populist and extremist ideas like never before. The trial has become a platform to promote his manifesto for the incoming general election of March 2017. The trial has become a weapon to fight even more the political establishment that is trying to *"silence him"*.

Can Wilders ever win and become Prime Minister? It is possible and it will all depend on whether the government will find new solutions and new measures to bring to the table for the voters to see and trust with regard to unemployment, the economy, and the migrant crisis.

If Wilders is to win the general election, because of the way politics work in the Netherlands with many small parties in parliament, he would still need to convince another political party, or maybe more than one, to work with him in order to build a majority through a coalition government. That would force him to moderate his stance on pretty much everything.

---

[62] Trump is a threat to the West as we know it, even if he loses (04/11/2016, Washington Post - https://goo.gl/PlFYpK)

Geert Wilders
@geertwilderspvv

CONGRATULATIONS @realDonaldTrump !!

Your victory is historic and for all of us!

#ElectionDay 🗳 #MakeAmericaGreatAgain

11:38 pm · 8 Nov 2016

* * *

"The real hate speech is not allowing free speech."

— Geert Wilders, 15 October 2016
(on Twitter)[63]

---

[63] Twitter, Geert Wilders (15/10/2016 - https://goo.gl/ewzoDc)

ITALY'S MANY FACES OF POPULISM.

- **Country:** Italy

- **Eligible to vote:** 42,271,967 (2013)

- **Next General election:** 23 May 2018

- **GDP:** $1.816 trillion (2015 est.)

- **Public debt:** 132.8% of GDP (2015 est.)

- **Unemployment:** 12.4% (2015)

- **Population below poverty line:** 29.9% (2012 est.)

- **Inflation rate:** 0.1% (2015 est.)

  (Source: The CIA World Factbook[64] & Eurostat[65])

KEY NAMES:

- **Silvio Berlusconi,** businessman, former Prime Minister, former leader of *Forza Italia*, a right-

---

[64] The World Factbook – Italy (Central Intelligence Agency - https://goo.gl/Ufz95s)
[65] Unemployment by sex and age - monthly average (Eurostat - https://goo.gl/3u7y2V)

```
wing political party.

   - Movimento 5 Stelle, or M5S, a left-
wing/right-wing ecologist, anti-establishment and
Eurosceptic political party.
```

We now turn to fascinating Italy. A country with a deep political tradition, but also the birthplace of some of the most troublesome populist characters and political movements.

For nearly a century, from Benito Mussolini's National Fascist party to Silvio Berlusconi's right-wing *Forza Italia* and Beppe Grillo's anti-establishment *Movimento 5 Stelle*, Italy seems to have been the theatre of a mighty political experiment, in which populism has unfortunately often rhymed with the self-delusion and the arrogance of political leaders who either led the country directly to the downfall of democracy or turned its economy into an utter failure. Let's take a look at the current situation.

Silvio Berlusconi.

Right-wing businessman Silvio Berlusconi served as Italy's Prime Minister for nearly 10 years thanks to his parties *Forza Italia* and *Il Popolo della Libertà* and thanks to his overall control of the media.[66] Berlusconi was elected on the promises that he would protect Italy from the Communists, that he would continue pro-Western free market policies and that his government would create *"one million more jobs"*. Berlusconi used his control over the media to launch massive campaigns of electoral advertisements. He who controls the media controls the minds.

Instead, Silvio Berlusconi's legacy will forever be his total failure to get Italy's economy to perform during all the years he was running the country, the promises that did not materialise and his trials for corruption, fraud and for paying an underage prostitute for sex.[67] It has also been claimed since that, while in charge of Italy's affairs, the *Cavaliere* largely benefited from enormous amounts of money and received presents from Vladimir Putin's Russia, in exchange for favours and influence.[68]

By reading what Italian pollster Nando Pagnoncelli of *Ipsos Italia*[69] had to say about Berlusconi's electorate in 2011: *"They are disproportionately old, live in small*

---

[66] Silvio Berlusconi, profile (Encyclopædia Britannica - https://www.britannica.com/biography/Silvio-Berlusconi)

[67] The cavaliere and the cavallo (09/06/2011, The Economist - http://goo.gl/6IjIMl)

[68] WikiLeaks cables: Berlusconi 'profited from secret deals' with Putin (02/12/2010, The Guardian - https://goo.gl/t7xb5X)

[69] Nando Pagnoncelli is the President of Ipsos Italia (@npagnoncelli)

towns, watch a lot of television, do not read newspapers, and don't believe there is any truth in accusations against the Prime Minister",[70] it is not difficult to draw comparisons between the former Italian Prime Minister and another rich businessman, the American Republican president-elect Donald Trump.

According to *The Economist, "The fundamental defect of Mr Berlusconi's governing style is that he often confuses private interests with public ones."* Providing that the two men have not only similar profiles but also similar objectives, this is something that should come as a worry with Donald Trump being elected President of the United States because the US are a far more powerful and influential country than Italy is.

Bloomberg has recently hinted at a possible comeback of the 80-year-old billionaire to politics in Italy.[71] Not as a Prime Minister, but as a kingmaker. He is said to be thinking about *"helping the current Prime Minister Matteo Renzi to change the electoral system to make it more favourable for setting up coalitions"* (and ultimately keep the rising left-wing/right- wing populist political party *Movimento 5 Stelle*, who Berlusconi sees as a threat that is

---

[70] The cavaliere and the cavallo (09/06/2011, The Economist - http://goo.gl/6IjIMI)
[71] Berlusconi Seen Poised for Comeback to Help Renzi After Vote (03/11/2016, Bloomberg - https://goo.gl/mBh7Wk)

channelling the anger of the Italians against their political elite, out of power), according to Francesco Galietti, head of political consultancy firm Policy Sonar.

Movimento 5 Stelle.

Another type of populism has surged since Berlusconi's exit, with the emergence in 2009 of the *Movimento 5 Stelle* (or *M5S*, Five Star Movement), both a left-wing and right-wing ecologist, anti-corruption, and Eurosceptic protest party, created by comedian Beppe Grillo.[72] In the 2013 general election, the party received 25.55 per cent of the votes, with 109 deputies and 54 senators.

M5S has become a growing force in Italy. It wants to organise a referendum on Italy's membership of the Eurozone in order to quit the Euro, not the European Union, therefore not an "Italexit", yet! The party also claims that greater public transparency is needed, an income support for the poorest and some tax cuts for small businesses as well.

It most recently took control of the cities of Turin with Chiara Appendino, 32, and Rome with Virginia Raggi, 37,

---

[72] Beppe Grillo, profile (Encyclopaedia Britannica - https://www.britannica.com/biography/Beppe-Grillo)

the first woman to ever hold the office of Mayor of Rome, on the promise to fight corruption and bring back Rome's splendour, after endless scandals were exposed about the previous administration (the city is roughly €13.6 billion in debt and counts more than 12,000 creditors, according to *Bloomberg*).[73]

In a recent post on the party's blog titled "The Games in Rome? No thank you!", a party Senator, Elio Lannutti, clearly explained that the *M5S* was against Rome hosting the 2024 Olympic Games (There are four candidates to host the Olympics in 2024: Rome, Paris, Budapest and Los Angeles).[74] *"No to cathedrals in the desert,"* the new Mayor of Rome said, knowing too well that the people of the capital were not very enthusiastic at the idea of the city hosting the Games and claiming that Rome would be left indebted and with redundant sports facilities.

That didn't go down too well with Giovanni Malago, the Italian Olympic chief, who then vowed to fight on, calling the mayor's decision *"demagogic and populist"*. To fight against Raggi's decision not to host the Games, the Italian Olympic Committee's social media accounts spent days

---

[73] Populist Politicians Take On Italy's Massive Debt Pile (07/07/2016, Bloomberg - http://goo.gl/BRk73y)

[74] Rome's populist 5-Star movement opposes 2024 Olympic bid (10/09/2016, France 24 - http://goo.gl/PkZ4kl)

defending the Italian bid through tweets and messages responding to the Mayor of Rome's arguments against Roma 2024, before the social media pages went "dark" on 2 October 2016 with a photograph of Rome in black and white.

"Not just Rome is a candidate, but the whole country is."[75]

"We lose an incredible opportunity for Rome and for Italy."[76]

---

[75] Twitter @Roma2024 - https://goo.gl/rOOhw3
[76] Twitter @Roma2024 https://goo.gl/WVzDCa

Roma 2024 @roma2024 · Oct 2
Il no a #Roma2024 è stato argomentato anche con il presunto debito
monstre delle Olimpiadi di #Roma60, ma in realtà...

*"The case for the NO to 'Roma 2024' was argued with the alleged
monster-debt of 'Roma 1960' Olympics, but the truth is...
it refers to about 2,000 practices from 1950 to 1990."*[77]

The Olympic Games controversy was not the only topic
Raggi found herself in trouble with after being elected
mayor. She, for instance, chose a head of environment who
was under criminal investigation and denied knowing
about it, before eventually admitting she had been made
aware of the situation. In politics, the "deny-deny-deny-
and-then-admit" strategy demonstrates inconsistency, a
fundamental lack of courage to confront accusations and,
most importantly, an appalling lack of transparency from a
politician who gets elected on the very idea of transparency,
on honesty and anti-corruption promises.

This is providing the stick to be beaten with. Prime

---

[77] Twitter @Roma2024 - https://goo.gl/BC1aG9

Minister Matteo Renzi didn't take long to react and ridicule *M5S*, saying: *"I have never seen so many lies one after the other"*.

It is finally important to note that, at the European Parliament, where it has 17 MEPs, *M5S* is openly affiliated to the Europe of Freedom and Direct Democracy group – chaired by one of the "Brexit-makers", Nigel Farage, together with far-right and anti-immigration parties such as Britain's UKIP, the Swedish Sweden Democrats, the Polish KORWiN and the German *Alternative für Deutschland*. That odd affiliation with openly far-right and racist parties makes some commentators describe M5S as either right-wing, far-right, both or even a fascist movement.

Conclusion.

Contrary to the situation in the United States with Donald Trump's candidacy to the White House in 2016, the days of a Berlusconi-like populist billionaire larger-than-life character, in Italy, are of a bygone age. Gone are the days when Italian politics meant that one man could control the media and be in charge of the country at the same time, would run the country the way he had run his business empire or would be more interested in fake tans and pool parties than in the country's failing economy.

The Guardian @guardian

Beppe Grillo provokes outrage with Sadiq Khan 'bomb' joke
trib.al/XG4ut6f

11:19 PM - 15 May 2016

Beppe Grillo provokes outrage with Sadiq Khan 'bomb' joke
Opponents criticise leader of Italy's Five Star Movement after he makes suicide bomber jibe about new London mayor
theguardian.com

Having been convicted of tax fraud by the Supreme Court and having received a public office ban, Berlusconi left a vacuum behind him. Not for long. *Movimento 5 Stelle* emerged and started to grab people's desire for another type of politics. However, because of the way some of its members tend to behave at the Chamber of Deputies, as well as the verbal violence and the use of famous mottoes from the Fascist era and the way some of its members or most senior leaders also make misogynist or racist remarks on social media, at political rallies or other events (Beppe Grillo's appalling suicide bomb joke on stage about the new Mayor of London, Sadiq Khan, was just one of such remarks), there are still doubts about whether *M5S* is indeed capable of inspiring people for a real change in Italy. A recent opinion poll shows that *M5S* would reach 29.6 per cent of the votes in a general election,[78] almost neck and neck with the ruling Democratic Party (31.8 per cent) of former Prime Minister Matteo Renzi, who resigned after his failed referendum on constitutional reform on 4 December 2016[79] that mostly became a plebiscite on the prime minister himself, rather than on the question on the ballot paper.[80]

However, now that *M5S* members have reached the Italian Parliament and even taken power in a couple of city halls, it looks increasingly as if the party, like most similar neo-anti- establishment movements born out of street protests and people's disappointment at mainstream parties, is learning a painful lesson: that with great power comes great responsibilities. It is indeed easier to be a loud, street-protest, pro-transparency, and anti-establishment

[78] Sondaggi politici 2016 / News elettorali, intenzioni di voto (28/09/2016, ilsussidiario.net - https://goo.gl/Zn2C5l)

[79] A great big reform package (08/10/2016, The Economist - https://goo.gl/owPytV)

[80] Fears mount that Renzi may be next referendum casualty (06/10/2016, The Guardian - https://goo.gl/uU9Xwe

movement than it is to be part of the establishment, being judged for your record, your deeds, rather than for your populist promises.

* * *

"According to a survey,
when asked if they would like to have sex with me,
30 per cent of women said, 'Yes',
while the other 70 per cent replied, 'What, again?'"

— Silvio Berlusconi, 31 March 2011
(Press conference in Lampedusa)[81]

[81] 'You deserve Nobel Peace Prize': Berlusconi praises Italian islanders outnumbered by Libyan and Tunisian immigrants (31/03/2011, Daily Mail - https://goo.gl/SM45lj)

WILL *PODEMOS* BETRAY THE SPANISH WORKING CLASS?

- **Country:** Spain

- **Eligible to vote:** 36,520,913 (2016)

- **Next general election:** 26 July 2020

- **GDP:** $1.2 trillion (2015 est.)

- **Public debt:** 93.9% of GDP (2013 est.)

- **Unemployment:** 22.7% (2015)

- **Population below poverty line:** 21.1% (2012 est.)

- **Inflation rate:** -0.5% (2015 est.)

(*Source: The CIA World Factbook[82] & Eurostat[83]*)

KEY NAMES:

---

82 The World Factbook - Spain (Central Intelligence Agency - https://goo.gl/pkGF7R)
83 Unemployment by sex and age - monthly average (Eurostat - https://goo.gl/3u7y2V)

- **Podemos**, or *Unidos Podemos*, a far-left political party.

- **Pablo Iglesias Turrión**, political scientist, far-left politician, leader and founder of *Podemos*.

Next stop in our exclusive reporting on the way populism has been spreading in the world in recent years: Spain. An intriguing and passionate country that flourished with mixed characters and a variety of cultures from the start.

The Celtic and Iberian populations were first Romanised, then the Peninsula was conquered by the Muslims. With the Kingdom of Castile that succeeded came political intrigues and infighting for power and influence, the Spanish Inquisition and Hernán Cortés's *Conquistadores*. The Spanish Empire was the first on which it was said that the sun never set.

Then, a gradual decline led to Spain being economically ruined and politically unstable, with endless fights over the succession leading to wars under the Napoleonic regime.

In 1939, after three years of civil war, General Francisco Franco, supported by Nazi Germany and Fascist Italy, became a dictator. It was not before his death, 40 years later, that democracy was finally restored in Spain.

The country, which is still quite a recent democracy, has two major political parties that have been in power at turns. But people's unhappiness, recession, high unemployment rate, austerity measures, inequality and popular anger over political scandals have led to see the rise of a new Spanish far-left. Unlike France or Greece, the far-right has made little ground in Spain. Instead, voters have been supporting a different type of populist political movement: *Podemos*.

Podemos.

Podemos ("We Can") is an anti-capitalist and anti-establishment movement that rose to fame almost overnight in 2014 thanks to its revolutionary message and its particular smart use of social media. It is now also known as *Unidos Podemos* ("United We Can") since its recent merging with the communists of *Izquierda Unida* ("United Left") and other smaller left-wing parties.

Within a year of existence, *Podemos* became the third largest party in the Spanish parliament, after receiving 20 per cent of the votes at the general election of December 2015 and controlled city halls across Spain.

On 18 October 2014, during the party conference in

Madrid, one of the party leaders, Pablo Iglesias Turrión, told supporters: *"El cielo no se toma por consenso, se toma por asalto!"* (*"You don't conquer heaven by consensus, you storm it!"*).[84] Storming heaven... A powerful slogan that he actually borrowed from... Karl Marx.

In his account of the civil war in France in April 1871, when the workers of Paris (then known as the "Communards") tried to overthrow the French government, Marx indeed wrote to Louis Kugelmann, his confidant, that *"the present rising in Paris – even if it be crushed by the wolves, swine and vile curs of the old society – is the most glorious deed of our Party since the June insurrection in Paris. Compare these Parisians,* **storming heaven,** *with the slave to heaven of the German- Prussian Holy Roman Empire..."*[85]

"Storming heaven" was also earlier mentioned in a book, *Hyperion,*[86] by Friedrich Hölderlin, a German lyric poet who was commonly associated with Romanticism and of whom Karl Marx is said to have been a fan.[87] In his book *Classical Horizons: The Origins of Sociology in Ancient Greece,* George E. McCarthy, a professor of sociology at

---

[84] Pablo Iglesias (18/10/2014, YouTube - https://youtu.be/4OssxceqDa4?t=40s)
[85] Marx-Engels Correspondence 1871 (Marxist.org - https://goo.gl/cgBBBr)
[86] Hyperion and Selected Poems (Google Books - https://goo.gl/Rk82s8)
[87] Friedrich Hölderlin, profile (Encyclopædia Britannica - https://www.britannica.com/biography/Friedrich-Holderlin)

Kenyon College in Ohio, says of Marx: *"Trained in classical Greek history and philosophy from his earliest days at the Trier Gymnasium and at the Universities of Bonn and Berlin, Karl Marx incorporated his love for ancient history, archaeology, and philosophy throughout his writings on political and economic issues."*[88]

By paraphrasing Karl Marx on that day of 2014, at the start of the *Podemos* "adventure", Iglesias purposely infused, injected *Podemos's* soul with a deep hard-left and Marxist sentiment. A connection that, far from the discourses of mainstream parties, could resonate with the audience on a very emotional level.

However, over time, the party leaders have been perceived by their supporters as not having worked enough on practical solutions to austerity and having extensively discussed ideologies instead.

What happened next was cold as stone: at the next general election, six months after their amazing result, they finished third again behind the two major parties, the *Partido Socialista Obrero Español* (PSOE, Spanish Socialist Workers' Party) and the conservative *Partido Popular* (PP, Popular Party), with 21 per cent of the votes,

---

[88] Classical Horizons: The Origins of Sociology in Ancient Greece (Google Books - https://goo.gl/QEFfxS)

gained no new seats at the parliament and, most tragically, lost over a million votes.

Another explanation for the sudden halt in *Podemos*'s rise was the fact that many supporters got upset at the sudden concentration of power in the hands of one man in particular, the party leader Pablo Iglesias Turrión, which they saw as a betrayal of their original stance on being a democratic social movement.

The powerful populist leader of *Podemos* is a delusional politician who takes Hugo Chavez's Venezuela and Latin America's hard-left leaderships as models for Spain and for Europe. Iglesias once shared his nostalgia of Hugo Chavez live on a Venezuelan government-controlled TV channel when watching an old recording of the former president of Venezuela.[89]

With its populist leadership, *Podemos* is on a dangerous path. Internal wars now oppose two types of leadership and ideologies: the anti-capitalist radicals and the more centre ground moderates. The party leadership also faces opposing regional memberships and various strategies that supporters would like the party to adopt. *"Both Errejón* [MP, number 2 of *Podemos* and one of the most visible

---

[89] Pablo Iglesias: "Los que simpatizamos con el Proceso Bolivariano" (04/07/2014, YouTube - https://youtu.be/RS8lesKPfl8?t=16m35s)

faces of the party] *and Iglesias* [number 1] *are revolutionaries. They ultimately have the same goal. The question is: how do you get to the revolution,"* explains sociologist and political analyst Jorge Galindo.[90]

According to *The Financial Times* journalist Tobias Buck, *"for* Podemos *to become a party of government,* [analysts] *argue, it must extend its appeal across the political spectrum, while keeping its core base of far-left voters on side."*[91]

Podemos does not try to reach out to the centre and concentrates too much on its core base instead. When some in the party did try to adopt a more liberal discourse to appeal to the centre, the attempts were immediately shut down by the most radical elements within the party, increasingly giving off the impression of a political movement that is far too revolutionary to ever be able to enter into government and that could potentially threaten the stability of the country.

The party's relationship with the Bolivarian Government of Venezuela, in particular, has been the subject of various controversies in Spain: donations,

---

[90] Jorge Galindo, Profile (Politikon - http://politikon.es/author/jorgegalindo/)
[91] Podemos still waiting to conquer Spain (18/10/2016, Financial Times - https://goo.gl/9aW1EF)

support, funding, deep admiration for Hugo Chávez... Íñigo Errejón once described Venezuela as his *"adopted fatherland"* and said he was a great supporter of Hugo Chávez. In November 2013, in an interview he gave to a Venezuelan government newspaper, *Correo del Orinoco*, the young MP even claimed that the lines for food Venezuelans were forced to experience for hours were there *"because they have more money to consume more"* and that they supposedly enjoyed socialising in the queues.[92]

Libertad Digital ✔
@libertaddigital

Errejón: en Venezuela hay colas porque "tienen más dinero para consumir más"
libremercado.com/2016-05-25/ini ... vía
@libre_mercado #PodemosEsChavismo

Íñigo Errejón: en Venezuela hay colas porque tienen "más d...
El número dos de Podemos ofrece tres argumentos surrealistas para explicar la existencia de largas colas en Venezuela, a cada cual más sorprendente.
libremercado.com

1:21 pm - 25 May 2016

In Venezuela, there are queues because
"they have more money to consume more"

On 22 October 2016, *Podemos*'s last hopes for a

---

[92] Íñigo Errejón: "En Venezuela hay colas porque tienen más dinero para consumir más" (26/05/2016, OK Diario - https://goo.gl/LiNXiV)

third general election in a year to take place which could have tested their chances to reach power in Spain once again were smashed into pieces when, after ten long months of discussions and fierce internal opposition that even led to the violent removal of the Socialist Party's own leader, the PSOE finally agreed to the Popular Party (PP) running the country with a minority conservative government led by Mariano Rajoy, the current prime minister.[93]

The PSOE didn't offer a blank cheque to Rajoy because they thought he was the right man for the job, they tried to avoid a third election that could have had the potential effect of drastically reducing their number of seats in parliament after months of infighting in the party. Indeed, between the last two elections in Spain, Rajoy's party was the only one that managed to increase its vote and number of seats.

"The PP may be looking to dissolve parliament to call a fresh election. That could happen as early as May 2017 – as soon as is constitutionally possible. Rajoy sees a chance to secure a more stable share of the vote and even to form a majority government," explains Paul Kennedy, a

---

93 Spain's Socialists vote to allow Rajoy minority government (23/10/2016, BBC News - https://goo.gl/rl4WcG)

lecturer in Spanish and European Studies at the University of Bath.[94]

Conclusion.

What does the future hold for *Podemos*? The party has attracted a lot of young voters who see the mainstream parties as representing the interests of the older generations in the country and now *Podemos* is at a crossroad. If it does go back to basics and reconnects with the working class and the social movement it came from, its supporters may come back and the party could win again. However, by confining itself to a radical left-wing ideology with a Bolivar-inspired rhetoric, it will also lose its only opportunity to grow any further by reaching out to the centre of the political spectrum. *Podemos* could end up institutionalising itself and could simply become a useless left- wing protest vote that would have lost any chance to ever lead a Spanish government because of its total inability to reach out to the middle classes.

On the other hand, if *Podemos* reaches out to the centre ground, while it will gain in opportunities to eventually join a minority government in the future with the PSOE, it will

---

[94] The messy politics behind Spain's new government (02/11/2016, The Conversation - https://goo.gl/aNB7pd)

totally lose its core radical supporters who will claim that the party has corrupted its original message, sold its values, and lost its soul, and become just another political party that is fully part of the very establishment it was meant to be fighting, like Greece's Syriza.

"Lo que le hace daño a nuestra democracia son quienes rinden nuestra soberanía a Alemania" @ierrejon

2.48 am - 23 Oct 2016

"Those who hurts our democracy are the ones who give our sovereignty to Germany," says Íñigo Errejón.

* * *

*"The Latin American model (Maduro's Venezuela,
Correa's Ecuador and Morales' Bolivia)
could be an alternative for Europe."*

— Pablo Iglesias, 24 June 2014
(Interview to *VTV*)[95]

---

[95] Video documento que expone la Venezuela descrita por Pablo Iglesias Turrión y Juan Carlos Monedero. (04/07/2014, YouTube.com - https://goo.gl/czaTk1)

DOES ANTI-AUSTERITY STILL MEAN ANYTHING IN SYRIZA'S GREECE?

- **Country:** Greece

- **Eligible to vote:** 9,840,525 (2015)

- **Next General election:** 20 October 2019

- **GDP:** $195.3bn (2015 est.)

- **Public debt:** 177% of GDP (2015 est.)

- **Bailout loans:** $271bn (2015 est.)

- **Unemployment:** 25% (2015)

- **Population below poverty line:** 36% (2014 est.)

- **Inflation rate:** -1.1% (2015 est.)

(Source: The CIA World Factbook[96] & Reuters[97])

---

[96] The World Factbook - Greece (Central Intelligence Agency - https://goo.gl/pVYuql)
[97] How much Greece owes to international creditors (28/06/2015, Reuters - https://goo.gl/wkaKwT)

KEY NAMES:

- **SYRIZA**, a radical-left political party.
- **Alexis Tsipras**, Prime Minister of Greece, leader of Syriza.

Our exclusive reporting on populism in the world continues with Greece, the birthplace of democracy.[98] Western civilisation owes nearly everything to Greece from modern politics to philosophy, literature, arts, and scientific thought.

It was, therefore, only logical that Greece would be the birthplace of a growing radical change in politics, a challenging thinking that led to an unconventional radical-left party running the country since 2015 and leading the way to other similar radical movements to grow all across Europe. But what have we actually learnt so far from Greece's "Syriza experiment"?

Syriza.

Syriza (a Greek syllabic abbreviation for "Coalition of the Radical Left") was originally founded in 2004 as a very eclectic coalition of green and left-wing parties and social/citizen/activist movements (including Maoists,

---

[98] Greece: Birthplace of the modern world? (07/11/2010, The Guardian - https://goo.gl/xPCBIA)

Eurocommunists, left socialists, ecologists, Marxists, and Trotskyites). According to the party's website,[99] *"Syriza draws inspiration from the progressive anti-neoliberal changes in Latin America and promotes close relations with many left forces in that region including with the São Paulo Forum."*[100] Something they have in common with Spain's *Podemos*, as we have already explained in the previous chapter.

The left-wing anti-austerity radical party gradually benefitted from the deepening radicalisation in Greece that started with the "Indignant Citizens Movement", a set of non-violent protests that lasted three months, between May and August 2011, and that took place throughout the country. The people of Greece protested against years of austerity, political turmoil, corruption, and behind-the-scene negotiations taking place between the Panhellenic Socialist Movement (PASOK) and the centre-right *Nea Dimokratia* (New Democracy, ND) after and during both the Great Recession of 2007[101] and the Greek debt crisis that followed.[102] The largest demonstration on 5 June gathered up to 300,000 people in front of the Greek Parliament. Amid a violent police crackdown, the square was eventually evacuated before new demonstrations took place again later.

---

[99] Who we are (Syriza - https://goo.gl/F8ifpw)
[100] Foro de Sao Paulo (Wikipedia - https://goo.gl/zCRcLH)
[101] What's a Global Recession? (22/04/2009, Wall Street Journal - https://goo.gl/mP4mSK)
[102] The Greek Depression (09/01/2013, Foreign Policy - https://goo.gl/z80wg)

After Socialist Prime Minister George Papandreou[103] offered to resign in November 2011, a national-unity coalition government was created with Lucas Papademos, an economist,[104] as Prime Minister. Papademos immediately explained that in order to facilitate the financial bailout from the European Union and keep Greece within the Eurozone, his government would have to implement new austerity measures on the country, i.e. substantial cuts in workers' income, minimum wage adjustments, abolition of Christmas and summer holiday bonuses, abolition of automatic wage increases...

By the time the May 2012 general election was held, the Greek voters had had enough of the government's endless austerity and the promises of even more austerity measures to come. Syriza, led by MP Alexis Tsipras,[105] had gained enough popular support to reach 16.8 per cent of the votes – four times its result of 2009. One million voters took 52 Syriza candidates to the Hellenic Parliament because of their anti-austerity and anti-capitalism stance, their demands for Greek government debts to be written off and their refusal to pay

---

[103] George Papandreou, profile (Encyclopaedia Britannica - https://www.britannica.com/biography/George-Papandreou)
[104] Lucas Papademos, profile (Encyclopaedia Britannica - https://www.britannica.com/biography/Lucas-Papademos)
[105] Alexis Tsipras, profile (Encyclopaedia Britannica - https://www.britannica.com/biography/Alexis-Tsipras)

Greece's creditors.

With its 52 newly elected MPs, it became the second largest party in parliament behind New Democracy. However, the negotiations between parties to form a government failed and Greece was forced into having a snap general election a month later.

Syriza's populism and irrationality started to show between the two general elections. The radical Greek party explained that *"[it] drafted a government program on the basis of which it fought the elections of 17 June 2012 with the visible possibility of being elected the first party. However, it has met with fierce reaction from the domestic establishment and European circles, who mounted a fear-mongering campaign against Syriza to terrorize the Greek people, in order to stop Syriza becoming the first, through parliamentary elections, left government in Greek history."*[106]

Those excessive and irrational fears echoed what American historian Richard Hofstadter[107] called *"paranoid delusions of conspiracy by the Money Power"*,[108] when he described the 1890s radical left-wing American People's

---

[106] Who we are (Syriza - https://goo.gl/4nXmTf)

[107] Richard Hofstadter, profile (Encyclopaedia Britannica - https://www.britannica.com/biography/Richard-Hofstadter)

[108] Populism: A Semantic Identity Crisis, by George B. Tindall (October 1972, Virginia Quarterly Review #48 - http://www.vqronline.org)

Party.[109] The populist movement was a reactionary anti-capitalism party that was hostile to mainstream parties, elites, banks, and cities. Its leaders were also running global conspiracy theories and seeking an idyllic past that never existed. Ring a bell?

Instead of deterring the voters, the groundless claims, together with Syriza's populist pledges to withdraw all Greek troops abroad, quit NATO and reduce military spending, only contributed to the increase of the party's share of the vote on 17 June 2012. With over 1.6 million votes (26.9 per cent) and 71 MPs, Syriza became the main opposition to the new national-unity coalition government led by New Democracy (29.8 per cent) and one step closer to reaching power in Greece.

In July 2013, Alexis Tsipras was confirmed as leader of Syriza, but infighting within the party meant he was then facing a growing movement that secured 30 per cent of the seats in the party's central committee. One of their main demands was for the party to keep open the possibility of Greece leaving the euro.

At the 2014 European election, Syriza finished first with 26.5 per cent of the votes, leaving New Democracy behind

---

[109] People's Party, profile (Encyclopaedia Britannica - https://www.britannica.com/event/Populist-Movement)

with only 22.7 per cent. This was the start of the end for the main political parties in Greece. In their own gloomy words, *"Syriza's main goal was to bring down the government and call for general elections, in order to end the modern Greek tragedy that the Greek people are living through."*[110]

A new general election eventually took place on 25 January 2015 in which Syriza grabbed more than 2.2 million votes (36.3 per cent) and 149 out of 300 seats in parliament, only two seats short of a majority. After forming what can only be described as an odd alliance with the right-wing conservative Party of Independent Greeks (ANEL) – an openly anti-liberal, anti-multiculturalism, anti-immigration, and pro-Greek Orthodoxy political party, in order to reach a majority, Alexis Tsipras became the new Greek Prime minister.

Whilst fellow leftist leaders congratulated Tsipras all over Europe, including *Podemos*'s Pablo Iglesias, in Brussels, the new Greek Prime Minister's choice of coalition partners immediately created some concerns for the Eurozone's finance ministers.[111] Concerns that could easily be conveyed by the words of economics analyst Wolfango Piccoli,[112] who told *Bloomberg*: *"The Independent Greeks are a conspiracy-*

[110] Who we are (Syriza - https://goo.gl/Fcl2xZ)
[111] Brussels fears tough line from Tsipras (26/01/2015, The Guardian - https://goo.gl/1RzLlG)
[112] Wolfango Piccoli (Teneo Intelligence - https://goo.gl/TCCGVq)

prone nationalist party... It's a bad mix, let's put it that way."[113] To describe the questionable coalition, Piccoli explained: *"This is a coalition of strange bedfellows because apart from the anti-austerity approach, these are two parties that are ideologically very divided. One is extreme left, the other is extreme right, they share no views at all together concerning issues like migration, like citizenship, so the glue is just about anti-austerity."*

There were concerns too for Europe's defence and security chiefs because of the increasingly apparent links between Syriza and Russia. Anton Shekhovtsov, a researcher who studies far-right politics in Europe, told the *Financial Times* that with Tsipras in power, *"Russia will certainly be looking to capitalise on the win of Syriza and pro-Kremlin sentiments that are fairly widespread in Greek society but especially in these parties. Their foreign policy is overtly, openly pro- Russia. And the fact that the new government's Prime Minister's first contacts were with the ambassador of Russia in Greece* [The first foreign official Tsipras invited to the Maximos Mansion in Athens was indeed Andrey Maslov, Russia's ambassador], *that means probably they will be trying to establish more significant cooperation with*

---

[113] Independent Greeks: Who are Syriza's right-wing coalition partners and what do they want? (26/01/2015, The Independent - https://goo.gl/iwnVVH)

Russia."[114]

So, barely had he got his feet under his new prime ministerial desk than Tsipras went to visit his new friend, Vladimir Putin. On 8 April, just three months after Syriza's win, the Greek Prime Minister and the Russian President met in Moscow and announced, not financial aid, but an agreement to boost cooperation in trade, tourism, and energy between the two countries. And maybe the promise of a lucrative gas deal too with a gas pipeline project.[115] Whatever the reason, the visit *"could not have come at a better time"*, Putin said at a press conference,[116] whilst Tsipras openly criticised the sanctions imposed by the West against Russia as *"a road to nowhere. This is our point of view that we constantly express to our colleagues in the EU. We don't think that this is a fruitful decision. It's practically an economic war."*

In Brussels, Guy Verhofstadt, the outspoken MEP and former Prime Minister of Belgium, publicly expressed his disapproval of the meeting on Twitter: *"The Greek Prime Minister should stop trying to play Putin against the EU. Putin cannot save Greece, the EU can."*

---

[114] Alarm bells ring over Syriza's Russian links (28/01/2015, Financial Times - https://goo.gl/iq81Fv)

[115] Putin tempts Tsipras with promise of lucrative gas deals… but can Russia really save Greece's skin? (08/04/2015, The Independent - https://goo.gl/tAepr5)

[116] Putin: Greece did not seek financial aid from Russia (08/04/2015, BBC News - https://goo.gl/RwpU4L)

Guy Verhofstadt ✔
@GuyVerhofstadt

The Greek Prime Minister should stop trying to play #Putin against the EU. Putin cannot save #Greece, the EU can #Tsipras

7:37 AM - 8 Apr 2015

Alexis Tsipras ✔
@tsipras_eu

Meeting with Russian President, @PutinRF_Eng ahead of this afternoon's press conference. #Greece

12:14 PM - 8 Apr 2015

The visits and "communications" between the two leaders didn't stop since. At the beginning of 2016, Russia even expressed a great interest in purchasing a Greek railway company and Greece's second-largest port, in Thessaloniki – so the Russians have direct access to the Mediterranean, thus avoid the narrow strait of the Bosporus that runs through the city of Istanbul, Turkey, Russia's "friendly, not so friendly!" enemy. What definitely worries the European Union and NATO is that the two countries now also talk about defence cooperation and weapons projects.[117]

Two peculiar anecdotes involving the Greek Prime Minister, reported by the *Financial Times* and two journalists of *Le Monde*, show how deep the Greco-Russian relationship seems to be.

The first anecdote, reported by the *Financial Times*, relates what happened during a NATO dinner in Poland, on 8 July 2016, with all 29 leaders of the Transatlantic Alliance attending.[118] During the dinner, the Greek Prime Minister urged his colleagues to end the stand-off with Russia and *"argued for partnership with Vladimir Putin."* On the closing session, US President Barack Obama slapped down Tsipras's position by saying *"We are united that there can be no business as usual with Russia. In good times and in bad, Europe can count on the United States. Always."* According to the Greek Defence minister Panos Kammenos, who confirmed the *FT* report, President Obama then told Tsipras:

[117] Is Russia's Alliance with Greece a Threat to NATO? (17/07/2016, National Interest - https://goo.gl/I0Qfyd)
[118] NATO show of unity masks domestic divisions (10/07/2016, Financial Times - https://goo.gl/Qiqm3s)

"This is something you ought to tell your friend Putin."[119]

The second anecdote comes from a recently published tell-all book written by two *Le Monde* journalists, *"A President Shouldn't Say That…"*, based on hundreds of hours of recorded interviews with France's President François Hollande.[120] In the book, the current president recounts the day Vladimir Putin called him (6 July 2015) to tell him that Greece had asked *"if Russia could print drachmas* [Greece's previous currency] *for them, because they didn't have the means to do it themselves in Greece."*[121] This surprising information means that Alexis Tsipras was at some point prepared to leave the Eurozone, which he had denied all along during the EU-Greece crisis that followed his election. Officials close to the Greek Prime Minister, however, denied he ever made such a request to Russia.

> «Je dois te donner une information (…). La Grèce nous a fait une demande d'imprimer les drachmes en Russie, car ils n'ont plus d'imprimerie pour le faire», aurait ainsi déclaré au téléphone Vladimir Poutine à François Hollande. «Je voulais te donner cette information, que tu comprennes bien que ce n'est pas du tout notre volonté», aurait-il ajouté.

Excerpt from the book *La Tribune de Genève*[122]

---

[119] Kammenos Says Obama Slapped Down Tsipras Over Putin (12/07/2016, National Herald - https://goo.gl/kUOv7N)
[120] Un président ne devrait pas dire ça… by Gérard Davet & Fabrice Lhomme (Amazon - http://amzn.to/2dPrmc8)
[121] Le livre de confidences de Hollande fait des vagues jusqu'à Athènes (14/10/2016, Le Figaro - https://goo.gl/FJ2XdP)
[122] Athènes dément des extraits du livre de Hollande (14/10/2016, La Tribune de Genève -

In June 2015, Alexis Tsipras presented a new proposal to deal with the Greek financial crisis and the country's international creditors with various measures and reforms that he thought all would agree to, but the EU Commission, the International Monetary Fund and the European Central Bank offered him a new bailout attached to a new set of conditions instead. Tsipras thought the Greek people should vote through a referendum whether to accept the offer or not. His recommendation was a "No" vote to give more strength to his government position.

In a way to sway the votes in his favour, and after the European Central Bank (ECB) said it would not increase emergency funding for Greek banks, the Prime Minister announced on 29 June, a few days before the referendum that banks and trading in Greek stocks would remain shut in order to impose capital control.[123] Greece was at risk to default and to exit from the Eurozone as its government was due to pay €1.6bn to the International Monetary Fund (IMF) on the same day its bailout was expiring.

With the Greeks queuing to withdraw a maximum of €60 per account per day and the banks remaining closed until two days after the referendum, Tsipras hoped he would become the people's champion and that a "No" vote would give him

---

https://goo.gl/5mVfzX)
[123] Greece shuts banks in bid to prevent collapse (29/06/2015, CNN - https://goo.gl/Ma0Sdp)

the momentum; he would have a clear mandate from his people to demand Greece's creditors write off 30 per cent of the country's debt and offer Greece a 20-year "grace" period during which it would not need to reimburse anything.

Speaking to an audience that had gathered in front of the Hellenic parliament, the Prime Minister said: *"On Sunday, we are not simply deciding to remain in Europe... We are deciding to live with dignity in Europe! I call on you to say 'No' to ultimatums and to turn the back on those who would terrorise you. No one can ignore this passion and optimism."*[124]

The result of the referendum was clear: "No" won with 61.3 per cent of the votes. Back at the negotiation table, a few days later, Tsipras agreed on a new loan of €82-86bn in exchange for a series of 49 austerity measures among which were: increase of the VAT, pension system reform, cut in public spending, revocation of government's laws, bank recapitalisation, privatisation of €50bn of state assets and decrease of public sector cost.

Oddly enough, the people of Greece voted to keep in power the populists of Syriza, whose anti-austerity government took them through a referendum for which they were asked to vote

---

[124] Greece PM urges 'No' vote to 'live with dignity in Europe' (04/07/2015, The Times of India - https://goo.gl/jz5K67)

against an austerity deal, before they eventually struck a controversial deal a week later that actually meant Greece would then face even more and tougher austerity measures than before.

On 14 August, the Greek parliament backed the new deal thanks to the vote of New Democracy and PASOK MPs, whilst Syriza was facing a rebellion of 40 MPs who voted against the deal. A week later, Tsipras resigned and called for a snap election, seeking a vote of confidence not from his own party, but from the Greek people. On 20 September, nearly 2 million voters chose to trust him once again (35.5 per cent) and gave Syriza 145 MPs in parliament (-4), which was enough to form yet another coalition government with ANEL's nationalists.

As Greek economic analyst Elias Ioakimoglou wrote in

Jacobin magazine: *"Syriza came to power in January 2015 with a mandate to resist the imposition of austerity. Instead, Syriza folded under the pressure of the troika, accepting intensified austerity measures and dashing the hopes of its supporters."*[125]

Thus, within weeks after Alexis Tsipras's second premiership began, the government faced a formidable backlash with farmers, doctors, pharmacists, port workers,

---

[125] Greece Was the Prologue (27/08/2015, Jacobin Magazine - https://goo.gl/6fpbk3)

civil servants and metro staff demonstrating in the streets because of the new set of measures.[126] This was Greece's first general strike since Syriza formed the government.[127]

And when on 17 November, Alexis Tsipras was heckled by anarchists who shouted anti-government and anti-austerity slogans as he attended a ceremony at a memorial for the 1973 student uprising against the military dictatorship,[128] he later compared the hecklers in parliament to far-right party Golden Dawn. A very unfair comment from the politician. The anarchists were likely among Syriza's core supporters if not voters, who since the beginning had faith in what was still a radical anti-establishment party and turned into a party of government instead, much like the conservatives of New Democracy or the socialists of PASOK. Tsipras's hecklers were likely among the people who had made Syriza possible and Alexis Tsipras Prime Minister of Greece.

In May 2016, the government passed in parliament yet more austerity measures, from tax increases to middle- and high-level income earners to the removal of VAT discounts, pensions cut, taxes increase on cigarettes, coffee, and craft beer... As well as calling for calm in the streets, the Prime

[126] Tsipras' biggest stress tests yet to come (02/11/2015, Reuters - https://goo.gl/oaN23x)
[127] Greece Comes to a Standstill as Unions Turn Against Tsipras (12/11/2015 – Bloomberg - https://goo.gl/8KGOwZ)
[128] Government officials heckled at Polytechnic wreath-laying (17/11/2015, Kathimerini - https://goo.gl/A64SEm)

Minister told the Greek people: *"Spring may be almost over but we are looking forward to an economic spring and a return to growth this year."* What if the expected growth did not materialise, whilst the austerity measures were increasing? What would happen to Greece?

Conclusion.

After having threatened the EU with a so-called "Grexit" over the Greek bailout agreement for a long time, Alexis Tsipras turned out to be more of a partner to Greece's creditors rather than an opponent. He indeed eventually imposed tougher austerity measures to the country. He also worked together with the other EU member states during the migrant crisis, which proved to be yet another great challenge for Greece. Hundreds of thousands of Syrian and Afghan refugees to deal with after they had risked their lives to get to Greece from Turkey in small boats.[129]

By reaching power in Greece, Tsipras's Syriza has become part of the establishment it once despised and shouted slogans against in the street. It has eventually worked together with the international creditors in the national interest with the short-term result that the Greek economy unexpectedly

---

[129] Migrants attempt sea crossing from Turkey to Greek island of Kos, in pictures (The Telegraph - https://goo.gl/jF1Xsq)

grew in the second quarter of 2016, successfully averting a recession.[130]

Bloomberg ✓
@business

Follow

Greece unexpectedly avoided a recession in 2nd quarter
bloom.bg/2aHcdba
12:34 PM - 12 Aug 2016

↩ ⇄ 45 ♥ 31

However, most of the 2 million people who voted for Syriza in the last 2015 general election and made it possible for the party to form a government are neither radical leftists nor Marxists or anti-capitalist activists, but ordinary people who did believe and had faith in the party's message and vision that a change from the establishment parties was possible. And these people are now angry because they think Syriza has lost its soul, lost its original message. A message that Alexis Tsipras rightly summed up in an interview he gave

---

[130] Greek Economy Grew Q2 (12/08/2016, Bloomberg - https://goo.gl/tEmDmn)

to the *New Statesman* in 2013, at a time when he was still probably only dreaming of becoming Prime Minister: *"I think this means that Syriza is not just a party with interesting positions, but a force that can bring change to the political landscape of Europe – not just for Greece, but for all the people who now need to reclaim their right to a decent society, justice and hope; against those who want to see them subjugated to this austerity that doesn't just kill wages and pensions, but democracy itself."*[131]

The problem is that as time passes, so does the chance of ending Syriza's very unpopular austerity project anytime soon. A time bomb is ticking... If the other two mainstream political parties, New Democracy [132] and PASOK, are unable to offer a different project, another plan that could somehow reduce the effect of austerity measures, to lift the pressure on the people and businesses, and save Greece's economy at the same time, the voters – or rather what will be left of voters – might end up turning to Golden Dawn, the neo-Nazi movement that emerged as Greece's third largest political force at the last general election with 6.28 per cent, to find more radical and more extreme solutions to sort the country.

---

[131] More and more people realise austerity is not viable. (19/03/2013, New Statesman - https://goo.gl/Nu2ONV)
[132] Mitsotakis' mission: Saving Greece from Tsipras (16/07/2013, Deutsche Welle - https://goo.gl/OtzGnh)

Alexis Papahelas,[133] the executive editor of Greece's daily newspaper *Kathimerini*, recently told *The Guardian*: *"Greece is for sure entering a new era and my great worry is that it could be very destructive."* The journalist added a warning: *"There are people in this country who know what war and occupation means but the young don't seem to know. My fear is that they may turn to an even more anti-systemic party, on the far right [in the event of failure]. I really don't rule it out."*[134]

* * *

---

[133] Alexis Papahelas (Politico - https://goo.gl/59fLkL)

[134] Syriza's Tsipras sworn in after Greek government formed with right-wingers (26/01/2015, The Guardian - https://goo.gl/nttNnE)

*"More and more people in Europe realise
that austerity is not a viable prospect.
I hope people realise that there is no other way
but to radicalise even further."*

— Alexis Tsipras, 19 March 2013
(Interview to the *New Statesman*)[135]

---

[135] More and more people realise austerity is not viable. (19/03/2013, New Statesman - https://goo.gl/EFw3JO)

AUSTRIAN NATIONALISM AND THE GLASS CEILING.

- **Country:** Austria

- **Eligible to vote:** 6,382,507 (2016)

- **Next Presidential election:** 4 December 2016

- **GDP:** $374.1 billion (2015 est.)

- **Public debt:** 86.2% of GDP (2015 est.)

- **Unemployment:** 5.7% (2015)

- **Population below poverty line:** 4% (2014 est.)

- **Inflation rate:** 0.8% (2015 est.)

(Source: The CIA World Factbook) [136]

KEY NAMES:

- **Norbert Hofer,** leader of the FPÖ, runner-up at the 2016 Presidential election.

---

[136] The World Factbook - France (Central Intelligence Agency - https://goo.gl/jV1epw)

- **FPÖ**, a far-right political party.

Norbert Hofer.

In May 2016, Norbert Hofer with his far-right political party *Freiheitliche Partei Österreichs* (FPÖ, Freedom Party of Austria) nearly created the surprise with the best result ever obtained by the leader of any nationalist party in Europe since the Second World War: runner-up with 49.65 per cent of the votes in the second round of the Austrian Presidential election. The FPÖ's anti-establishment, anti-immigration, anti-Islam and anti- Europe stance had nearly got Hofer to win the election.

The man *Business Insider* calls *"Austria's Donald Trump"* for his anti-immigration stance and his claims that the increase of gun ownership was linked to immigration – Hofer always carries a gun with him everywhere – was little known before suddenly reaching 35.1 per cent of the votes in the first round of the Presidential election, when his opponent in the second round, the Green Alexander Van der Bellen received only 21.3 per cent, a difference of over 500,000 votes. Yet in the second round, the gap didn't materialise into a win for Hofer.

The former aeronautical engineer, who also briefly served

as a guard on the Austrian border with Hungary, worked his way to the top of the Freedom Party of Austria where he became an advisor to Heinz-Christian Strache, the current Chairman of the far-right party. Then, in 2013, he became Third President of Austria's National Council, which essentially makes him one of two deputies to the Speaker of the country's Parliament.[137]

Hofer's image is the one of a polished, well-spoken, cultivated, friendly and moderate politician whose model is Margaret Thatcher (another one!). Such a portrait should not really fit within the far-right Freedom Party of Austria. Behind the smooth talk, however, Norbert Hofer promises to curb migration from outside of the EU, vows to deport Muslims because according to him *"Islam has no place in Austria"*,[138] says that he wants to hold a referendum on Austria's membership of the EU – so-called "Auxit" – and proposes that the territory of South Tyrol, formerly part of the Austro-Hungarian Empire (1867-1918) and now administered by Italy, should be absorbed into Austria. He is seen as a populist moderate because his discourse differs from verbal-abuse master Strache and also because Hofer can talk employment, economy, immigration, and security to the voters, broadening

---

[137] Ing. Norbert Hofer - Third President of the National Council (Parliament of Austria - https://goo.gl/EvYwzJ)

[138] Who are the two men who competed to be Austria's next president? (23/05/2016, The Guardian - https://goo.gl/OVwFtU)

the mass appeal and credibility of the FPÖ – like what Marine Le Pen did with the French *Front National.*

The combination of his "soft" nationalist style with his slogans *"Putting Austria first"* and *"Unspoilt, honest, good"* and the miraculous migrant crisis – with nearly 100,000 migrants applying for asylum in the country – paid off in the first round of the Presidential election, even though it was not enough to win in the second round, nor to win the re-run of the vote on 4 December 2016 that was eventually won by the Green-backed candidate Alexander Van der Bellen with 53.8 per cent.[139]

The election re-run had been yet another chance for Hofer to try to be the first to break the glass ceiling that has, so far, been unreachable even for the strongest nationalist party in Europe, Marine Le Pen's *Front National.* Shortly after the vote on 4 December, Le Pen took tweeted: *"Congratulations to FPO that fought with courage. The next parliamentary elections will be those of their victory."*

Marine Le Pen ✔
@MLP_officiel

Félicitations au FPÖ qui s'est battu avec courage. Les prochaines législatives seront celles de leur victoire ! MLP
4:41 PM - 4 Dec 2016

---

[139] Victory for Van der Bellen and the left (04/12/2016, The Guardian - https://goo.gl/u4B3sF)

On the night of the results, Norbert Hofer had only one person to blame for his defeat: Nigel Farage! Two days earlier, Farage had appeared on *Fox News* and had said that if elected president, Hofer would *"be calling for Austria to have a referendum on their membership with the European Union. The president of Austria being the head of state — not with much executive power, but still very important — I would put my money on the Freedom Party's Mr Hofer winning that election."*

Before the vote, Hofer had had to deny the claim and openly criticise Nigel Farage, describing his comment as *"a crass misjudgement"* before adding *"It doesn't fill me with joy when someone meddles from outside. I would ask Mr Farage not to interfere in Austria's internal affairs. It is not something I want* (a referendum on Austria's EU membership). *We need to build a stronger union."*

This certainly was an international political blow to Nigel Farage.[140]

Although Hofer failed in his attempt to become president, the fact remains that nearly half of the Austrian voters (46.2 per cent) were adamant in their desire to see him as their new president and backed him in the re-run of the election. A

---

[140] Austria's far-right Freedom Party blames Nigel Farage for election defeat (05/12/2016, International Business Times - https://goo.gl/8UH60j)

worrying sign for the General election that should take place by October 2018.

Conclusion.

Hofer would certainly like to have a destiny similar to the one of Hungarian Prime Minister Viktor Orbán who has managed to apply nationalist and ultra-protectionist policies in Hungary under his conservative right-wing banner. Austria too is a sharply divided nation and it has the potential to become one of the most intolerant member of the European Union.

The Austrian voters have shown that they did not learn anything from the first run of the Presidential election, or didn't want to be told that they had been wrong in voting for Hofer. The vote for Hofer had not merely been a rejection vote against the establishment, but also a vote of approval of Hofer's populism and extreme ideology. Even though he lost the same election twice, Norbert Hofer has managed to make the FPÖ a more mainstream party enough to reach out to an electorate that would never vote for the far-right party.[141]

The perspective of a far-right party reaching the top of the

---

[141] Norbert Hofer, the friendly face of the populist right (03/10/2016, Democratic Audit UK - https://goo.gl/1LEmXl)

political establishment in one of the 28 countries that currently composes the European Union, for the first time since World War II, is anything but what anyone with common sense should be looking forward to. It would absolutely set a very unfortunate precedent for future elections in the rest of Europe and would galvanise, as never before, the nationalists and populists of far-right political parties across the Continent.

That perspective should no longer be ignored and should be addressed as a matter of urgency, in Austria and in the rest of the EU.

Joe Klamar/Agence France-Presse — Getty Images

The New York Times ✔
@nytimes

Follow

Austria's far-right candidate Norbert Hofer has narrowly lost the presidential vote nyti.ms/20qR3Ny
4:05 PM - 23 May 2016

"For me, Austria is a nation.
But I won't condemn anyone who sees it differently."

— Norbert Hofer, 17 May 2016
(Interview to *Die Presse*)[142]

---

[142] Norbert Hofer: "Ist Integration noch möglich?" (17/05/2016, Die Presse - https://goo.gl/apOKVl)

HUNGARY'S MAINSTREAM ILLIBERAL POPULISM.

- **Country:** Hungary

- **Eligible to vote:** 8,272,625 (2016)

- **Next General election:** Spring 2018

- **GDP:** $120.6 billion (2015 est.)

- **Public debt:** 75.3% of GDP (2015 est.)

- **Unemployment:** 6.8% (2015 est.)

- **Population below poverty line:** 14.9% (2015 est.)

- **Inflation rate:** -0.1% (2015 est.)

(Source: The CIA World Factbook)[143]

KEY NAMES:

- **Viktor Orbán,** Prime Minister of Hungary, leader of *Fidesz.*

---

[143] The World Factbook - France (Central Intelligence Agency - https://goo.gl/jV1epw)

- *Fidesz,* a national conservative political party.

Viktor Orbán.

Aged only 53, Viktor Orbán has already been twice Prime Minister of Hungary, in 1998–2002 and again in 2010.[144]

Because of his populism, his Eurosceptic and nationalist views, Orbán has been called an "authoritarian", a "dictator", a "Putinist" and a "populist", and compared to politicians as diverse as Donald Trump, Recep Tayyip Erdoğan and Vladimir Putin. Whilst his national conservative party *Fidesz* (Hungarian Civic Alliance) has been compared to political parties such as Britain's Tories, France's *Front National* and Spain's *Podemos*.

In recent years, *Fidesz* obtained a couple of supermajorities at the parliament that gave Orbán all necessary powers to modify or change the country's laws and Constitution at will. The changes that took place in 2011 were heavily criticised[145] by the Council of Europe, the European

---

[144] Viktor Orbán, profile (Encyclopaedia Britannica
- https://www.britannica.com/biography/Viktor-
Orban)
[145] Q&A: Hungary's controversial constitutional changes (11/03/2013, BBC News -
http://goo.gl/RaLyMR)

Union [146] and the United States [147] mostly because of concerns regarding the centralisation of the legislative and executive power, the weakening of the Constitutional Court and the judiciary, the curbing of civil liberties, the restrictions on freedom of speech and the lack of transparency and lack of public debate during the drafting of the new Constitution.

In a 2014 speech he gave in Băile Tuşnad, Romania, Viktor Orbán explained that in his view, *"systems that are not Western, not liberal, not liberal democracies and perhaps not even democracies, can nevertheless make their nations successful."* He then went on citing Singapore, China, India, Russia and Turkey as models. [148]

Citing Russia, in particular, should have come as no surprise since Orbán's government had secured some large business with Moscow in January 2014, among which was the construction of two new controversial Russian-financed reactors at Hungary's only nuclear plant, making the country fully dependent on Russia for its electricity, as it was already regarding its oil and gas supply. [149]

---

[146] European Parliament resolution of 5 July 2011 on the Revised Hungarian Constitution (05/06/2011, European Parliament - http://goo.gl/0PRTbB)

[147] A Second Look - Op-Ed by Ambassador Eleni Tsakopoulos Kounalakis published in the Hungarian weekly Heti Válasz (08/12/2011, Embassy of the United States in Budapest - http://goo.gl/i5pbDp)

[148] Prime Minister Viktor Orbán's Speech at the 25th Bálványos Summer Free University and Student Camp (26/07/2014, Website of the Hungarian Government - http://goo.gl/reNKok)

[149] Hungarian MPs approve Russia nuclear deal (06/02/2014, BBC News - http://goo.gl/34nZEL)

Some critics said at the time that the real motive for the Russian financing of the atomic power station was to buy influence,[150] and indeed, since the Orbán-Putin deal was struck, not only had Hungary been criticising the EU's embargo on Russia, but it had clearly shifted its main foreign policy towards a friendlier attitude with the Kremlin, even daring to invite the Russian president on official bilateral visits. So? Is Russia buying influence or genuine alliance of interests? The exact details of the deal have been placed under a 10-year secrecy rule. History will judge.

What we do know though is that Viktor Orbán's rhetoric about asylum seekers arriving in Europe, coupled with the recent terrorist attacks that took place in the European Union and the idea that nationalist and protectionist policies are in his country's national interest, have been embraced by European mainstream conservative politicians.

By suggesting lately that *"every single migrant* [posed] *a public security and terror risk"*, describing their migration as *"not a solution, but a problem"* and *"not a medicine, but a poison"* and claiming that his country did not want or need *"a single migrant"*, Orbán literally opened Pandora's box.[151]

---

[150] Special Report: Inside Hungary's $10.8 billion nuclear deal with Russia (30/03/2015, Reuters - http://goo.gl/GxWV3E)

[151] Hungarian prime minister says migrants are 'poison' and 'not needed' (27/07/2016, The Guardian - https://goo.gl/YztoQp)

Together with other Eastern European countries such as Slovakia and Poland, Hungary categorically opposed accepting 1,294 refugees allotted to it through the European Union's 2015 resettlement scheme.[152]

To show his opposition to the EU scheme to relocate 160,000 refugees across member states, Orbán called a divisive referendum on the scheme on 2 October 2016.[153] The EU scheme was overwhelmingly rejected by 98 per cent of the voters – 3.3 million voters, but as only 40.4 per cent of eligible voters cast their ballots, after the successful boycott of the referendum by opposition parties and human right groups – far from the required 50 per cent threshold – it rendered the referendum result invalid.

Belgian MEP Guy Verhofstadt was quick to react to the referendum result on Facebook: *"It looks like Viktor Orban lost his bet; after an appalling campaign by the Government, today's referendum in Hungary on the admission of refugees is null and void as the required 50% threshold was not met. Hungarian citizens have showed today that they don't support and will not follow Orban's populist, xenophobic and racist policies."*[154]

---

[152] Enhancing legal channels: Commission proposes to create common EU Resettlement Framework (13/07/2016, European Commission - https://goo.gl/Mku1rG)

[153] Hungarian referendum: plurality rejects EU migrant plan, but poll numbers too low to be valid (02/10/2016, Deutsche Welle - https://goo.gl/HE2K2g)

[154] Guy Verhofstadt (02/10/2016, Facebook - https://goo.gl/rLV243)

Nevertheless, Viktor Orbán declared victory and even called a constitutional vote at the parliament. In a press conference, he told journalists: *"Thirteen years after a large majority of Hungarians voted at a referendum to join the European Union, today Hungarians made their voices heard again in a European issue. We have achieved an outstanding result, because we have surpassed the outcome of the accession referendum."*[155]

Orbán felt that he had earned the support of the

[155] Hungarians vote to reject migrant quotas, but turnout too low to be valid (03/10/2016, Reuters - https://goo.gl/MWIm38)

population through the referendum and, a week later, on 8 October, the journalists of Hungary's largest broadsheet and main opposition newspaper, *Népszabadság*, (People's Freedom) found their offices closed after it had been shut down without giving notice by the parent company, *Mediaworks* – itself acquired by *Opimus*, which is friendly with the *Fidesz* government of Viktor Orbán.

When asked by a *Byline* journalist what he made of the claim that the paper had been shut down for economic reasons, András Dési, a senior editor and reporter who worked at the paper for more than 26 years said: *"I don't believe any word of that."* He explained: *"You have to see the whole political context here in Hungary. First, we launched a series of investigative journalism stories about the corruption affairs and other affairs of people who are close to the prime minister."*[156]

It was not difficult to see how Orbán and his government were trying to take control of the media to strengthen *Fidesz*, like what happens in Putin's Russia. One voice, one line. No opposition to the ruling party.

"I think it was absolutely a politically motivated decision. We don't have any proof or evidence of that. But all signs

[156] Politics and the downfall of Népszabadság (27/10/2016, Byline - https://goo.gl/LkLgXz)

indicate that there is purely politics behind it. They are transforming the whole media landscape in Hungary and Népszabadság doesn't fit in."

As if taking control of the media wasn't enough, Orbán needed stirring things up as he was pushing the constitutional bill on refugees to parliament and, to galvanise his supporters, he gave an interview to a state radio on 28 October, in which he said in an openly anti-migrant fashion that *"there shouldn't be a large migrant community in Hungary, arriving from a foreign culture, let's state that clearly. That's our aim."*

Kenneth Roth @KenRoth

New racist state-issued school book asks Hungarian kids to "spot the Europeans." Viktor Orban at his intolerant best bit.ly/2dk4Bd5

3.2. ábra. **Népek kavalkádja**
Keresd meg az ábrán az európaiakat! Mely ismertető-jegyek alapján találtad meg őket?

1:44 am - 2 Oct 2016

Kenneth Roth, Executive Director, Human Rights Watch. (Twitter @KenRoth)[157]

On 8 November, however, the parliament rejected the bill to block the settlement of refugees in Hungary,[158] as his party failed to reach the two thirds majority of votes with only 131 MPs out of 199.[159] This, more than the invalid referendum, delivered a big bad blow to Viktor Orbán.

Conclusion.

Through his opportunism and his populist ideology, Viktor Orbán remains in power in Hungary, under the cover of being a "very" conservative politician. Certainly one of the most so-called "very conservative" politicians in the European Union.

His poisonous speech against migrants as well as his intolerance are now spreading and hailed as some kind of "truth" by many European populist politicians.

If his mainstream illiberal populist views reach a growing audience beyond the borders of Hungary, Viktor Orbán could be seen as the man responsible for leading to the possible demise of the European Union's motto, "Unity in diversity"[160], and ultimately, the demise of the EU itself. To the benefit of

---

[158] Hungarian Lawmakers Deal Blow to Prime Minister Viktor Orban's Migrant Plans (08/11/2016, Wall Street Journal - https://goo.gl/2rFisu)
[159] Hungarian Lawmakers Deal Blow to Prime Minister Viktor Orban's Migrant Plans (08/11/2016, Wall Street Journal - https://goo.gl/2rFisu)
[160] The EU Motto (Europa – The European Union - https://goo.gl/MJvgk2)

his good friend, Russian President Vladimir Putin...

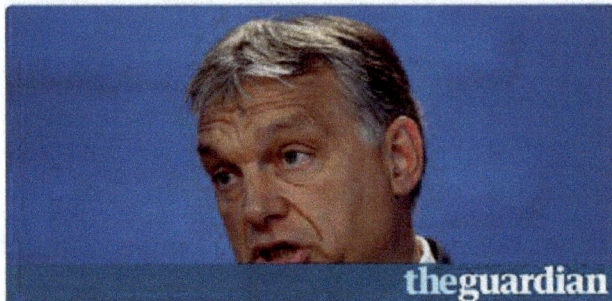

Sejal Parmar
@_SejalParmar

Follow

#Hungary's PM #Orban shrinks to new lows, saying migrants are 'poison' and 'not needed' theguardian.com/world/2016/jul...

2:06 PM - 27 Jul 2016

Hungarian prime minister says migrants are 'poison' and 'not ne...
The populist leader fuels anti-immigrant sentiment and praises Trump's foreign policy ideas as 'vital' for Hungary
theguardian.com

* * *

*"We have lost our media, the right-wing media
that helped the supporters of* Fidesz.
*There is a conflict between the government and
the owners of the dominant right-wing media.
That is the truth."*

— Viktor Orbán, 17 May 2016
(Interview to *Echo TV*)[161]

---

[161] Estranged from media mogul friend, Hungary PM seeks new allies (12/05/2015, Reuters - https://goo.gl/WU9cy2)

DANGEROUS
EUROPEAN POLITICS.

Far-left and far-right political parties are not a thing of the 21st century. They did not just suddenly pop out of nothing or nowhere. They have been around for some time, but had such a minor appeal to the mass public that they were absolutely insignificant on the political spectrum. They represented the end form of a radical movement that was not allowed to grow because it had nowhere to grow, for mainstream political parties were effectively occupying the entire political sphere.

But events such as corruption trials, financial crises, the migrant crisis, and terrorism, combined, have created the right recipe to get both the radical left and the radical right to awaken and get more and more support from the voters in every country of the European Union.

As described in our reports on France, the Netherlands, Italy, Spain, Greece, Austria and Hungary, there is a deeply radical movement that grows and spread across Europe. Germany, Denmark, the Czech Republic, and Poland have not escaped the trend. A number of violent attacks on asylum seekers or their reception centres have happened in Germany recently, for instance, and the anti-immigrant Alternative for Germany (AfD) has been gaining support. Populists such as Miloš Zeman in the Czech Republic and Andrzej Duda in Poland are definitely enjoying the momentum.

Dīvide et īmpera (divide and rule) could be the likes of Sarkozy, Le Pen, Trump and Farage's motto. As Niccolò Machiavelli wrote in *The Prince*, the aims of princes for glory and survival can justify the use of immoral means to achieve those ends.[162] When the populism virus spreads in the society, reality and facts absolutely lose all authority in politics. Whoever dares bring them back on the table belongs to the establishment, is involved in "Project fear", takes side with the experts. They are considered subjective and biased.

So, how do you make a populist character win?

You need a populist politician who will identify a very complex issue for the so-called "silent majority": unemployment, security, just name it. They will then find someone to blame for it and explain how they come up with a

---

[162] The Prince, by Niccolò Machiavelli (Amazon – http://amzn.to/2fnaW6x)

solution. The problem is that the solution will simultaneously win votes and make things worse for the country and therefore for the very people who voted for them.

Populists give voters someone they can/should blame for their life: migrants, Jews, Muslims, Mexicans...

Populists offer excuses, but never realistic plans: we will build a wall, we will check their teeth...

Why are populists popular? Because they give people a chance to blame someone else for their problems. The others. The foreigners. The aliens. The people who don't belong to this country.

"For the state must draw a sharp line of distinction between those who, as members of the nation, are the foundation and support of its existence and greatness, and those who are domiciled in the state, simply as earners of their livelihood there."

"Very important that firms declare how much of their workforce is foreign because they're just domiciled in this state simply as earners of their livelihood."

"They're not members of the nation, they're not members of the foundation and the support of the nation's existence and greatness."

These lines could have been written or spoken by any of the populist characters mentioned in this book, even by Donald Trump. Adolf Hitler wrote them in *Mein Kampf*.

It is quite unfortunate, to say the least, that many people forgot that Adolf Hitler reached power through an election after the German economy had collapsed. Whilst the mainstream political parties couldn't handle the terrible consequences of the financial crisis of 1929, Hitler offered angry people convenient scapegoats, pledged to restore law and order in Germany and also promised he would restore Germany's former greatness and glory. *"Make Germany Great Again"*, Hitler would certainly say today. The frustration was growing and people were so desperate for solutions and for hope that they decided to turn to the Nazi party.

Ring a bell?

Here we are. 2016.

The same ideologies, the same methods, the same speeches, the same solutions are spreading again.

Tongues are now loose and it suddenly seems all right for populist and nationalist politicians across Europe to use a once muted and underground far-right extremist and xenophobe language in the media, in political rallies and in election campaigns.

It now seems perfectly acceptable and even mainstream for them to poison the airwaves with their vile and racist language. It is not limited to the old Continent, though.

Didn't Donald Trump become the international symbol of the racist alt-right movement during his campaign in 2016, before he became President-elect of the United States? Was it not intended? Too late to be sorry now.

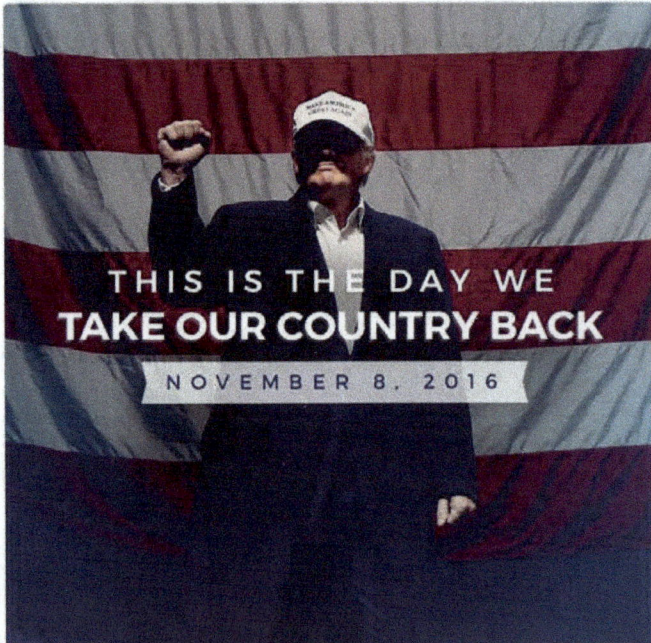

Official Team Trump ✔
@TeamTrump

Today is a historic day for us -- for OUR movement. Today is the day that we take back our country! #MakeAmericaGreatAgain

THIS IS THE DAY WE
TAKE OUR COUNTRY BACK
NOVEMBER 8, 2016

8:05 am - 8 Nov 2016

In the next volume in the series, *Populism in the Americas*, we will report on populism in Latin and South America with countries such as Brazil, Argentina and Venezuela and extensively report on Donald Trump's extreme and populist campaign during the 2016 US Presidential election that saw him defeat Hillary Clinton to head to the White House. We will explore the extent to which the Republican candidate's win may change the politics and the geopolitics across the world. If not Brexit, is President Trump the tip of the populist iceberg?

EU Elections 2016-2018.

What's next for Europe then? With the Brexit vote and the election of President Trump in 2016, we may wonder what else is still to come... What other unpredicted turn of event will we witness in the months to come? Don't ask the pollsters, they keep getting everything wrong!

-   **15 March 2017:** General election in the Netherlands. Could this be the opportunity for far-right Geert Wilders to finally become Prime Minister?

-   **7 May 2017:** Presidential election in France. Far-right Marine Le Pen would love to become the first woman president in France. Can any other politician upset her plans?

- **September/October 2017:** General election in Germany. It seems very unlikely that far-right Alternative for Germany could upset Angela Merkel in any way. Or, is it?

- **October 2018:** General election in Austria. Will the FPÖ confirm its very good result (although defeated) at the Presidential election and reach power with a far-right prime minister?

There is still one question that certainly deserves an answer: who could be the great beneficiary of both the US and the EU chaotic tragedies that currently unfold before our eyes with the sudden rise of populism, nationalism and alt-right/far-right parties and politicians?

A clue...

J.N. PAQUET ✍
@jnpaquet

From Russia, with love.

#TrumpPresident #ElectionNight 🏛
#Election2016 🏛 #Trump #Putin

"I will build a great wall – and nobody builds walls better than me, believe me – and I'll build them very inexpensively. I will build a great, great wall on our southern border, and I will make Mexico pay for that wall. Mark my words."

— Donald J. Trump, 16 June 2015
(Presidential Announcement Speech)[163]

BREXIT. THE TIP OF THE POPULIST ICEBERG?

ABOUT THE AUTHOR

J.N. PAQUET is the author of over 50 books and a journalist who has been covering France, Brazil, and Britain's current affairs for over two decades for several newspapers, magazines and websites in Taiwan, the US and the UK. He is currently a Political Writer for Byline and the Huffington Post UK.

His official website: **www.jnpaquet.co.uk**
Twitter: **@jnpaquet**

ISBN 9781911435020 (PAPERBACK)
eISBN 9781911435037 (EBOOK)

www.ingramcontent.com/pod-product-compliance
Lightning Source LLC
Chambersburg PA
CBHW072137020426
42334CB00018B/1844